34.95

DATE DUE

DEMCO

THE STRANGE CAREER OF
THE BLACK ATHLETE

THE STRANGE CAREER OF THE BLACK ATHLETE

African Americans and Sports

Russell T. Wigginton

Forward by Reverend Benjamin L. Hooks

Westport, Connecticut
London

Library of Congress Cataloging-in-Publication Data

Wigginton, Russell Thomas.
  The strange career of the black athlete : African Americans and sports / Russell T. Wigginton.
        p. cm.
  Includes bibliographical references and index.
  ISBN 0–275–98223–8 (alk. paper)
  1. African American athletes—History.   2. Sports—United States—History.
I. Title.
GV583.W547 2006
796.089' 96073–dc22   2006005771

British Library Cataloguing in Publication Data is available.

Library of Congress Catalog Card Number: 2006005771
ISBN: 0–275–98223–8

First published in 2006

Praeger Publishers, 88 Post Road West, Westport, CT 06881
An imprint of Greenwood Publishing Group, Inc.
www.praeger.com

Printed in the United States of America

The paper used in this book complies with the
Permanent Paper Standard issued by the National
Information Standards Organization (Z39.48–1984).

10 9 8 7 6 5 4 3 2 1

CONTENTS

PREFACE

Like most young African American boys at age 12, when someone asked me what I wanted to be when I grew up, I replied, "A professional basketball player." At the time this dream seemed like a real possibility. As a sixth grader in Louisville, Kentucky, I had led my parochial league team in scoring and I fancied myself as a pretty slick ball handler. Although I knew I probably was not likely to grow very tall (my dad is 5'8" and my mom is 5'3"), Tiny Archibald and Calvin Murphy had become stars in the National Basketball Association, and neither one of them had reached 6 feet tall. Plus I was a standout in Louisville, a place known for producing a disproportionate number of great basketball players for a city its size. But little did I know that my world as defined by sports was about to be turned on its head before I reached 13.

One day toward the end of my sixth grade school year, my father came home and announced that he had good news and bad news; the good news was that he had been offered a promotion at work, but the bad news was that the job was in Nashville, Tennessee. For a kid my age who thrived on routine and predictability, this news was devastating. Although I remembered my father being promoted and the family relocating earlier in my life, I recalled that the experience had been traumatic. When I was in the second grade, we moved from Louisville, Kentucky, to Evansville, Indiana. Although there is only approximately 125 miles between the two places, for a little black boy they were worlds apart. At the time of the move we were living in an overwhelmingly black community and had numerous family members from both parents' sides living in the same town. When we moved to Evansville, I recall seeing very few black people in the entire town, and I know I was the only black kid in the Catholic elementary school that I attended. Although I was quite young and recall very few incidents in which my race was much of a factor, I remember wondering if people really liked me, or if I was such a novelty that I was more like a toy or a pet than a friend. Fortunately we moved back to familiar surroundings after only two years. So when my dad announced that we were moving again, and this time farther south, I was very disturbed.

Being somewhat shy and an introvert at the time, I responded that summer before we moved by spending incredible amounts of time working on my basketball skills in my backyard and on the playground courts in the neighboring parks. I did this for two reasons: I knew my time to spend with my friends was limited and there was not a moment to waste. I had figured out that one way to gain instant popularity at my new school, whether or not I was going to be one of a handful of African American students, was to be a top-notch athlete. By now I had begun to believe in the idea that sport was the "equalizer" in society. People were always talking about how athletes, regardless of race, had to put their differences aside and work together if the team was going to be successful. And this was the late 1970s where you had more examples of interracial exchanges in most sports than at anytime in America's history.

The two black athletes that I admired the most at this time were Arthur Ashe and Kareem Abdul-Jabbar. Ironically, both were UCLA graduates, but in the eyes of the public they were extremely different. Ashe was thought of as soft-spoken, thoughtful, and a man of principle. Because of his demeanor, or perhaps because of the sport he played, tennis, Ashe seemed to make people feel comfortable around him. One of the biggest compliments paid to me when I was a boy was when a coach told me that he thought that I carried myself like a young Arthur Ashe. While I blushed and accepted his kind words, unbeknown to this coach, I admired Abdul-Jabbar as much as Ashe. Abdul-Jabbar was considered aloof, moody, and difficult to get close to by most people. Perhaps he was all of those things, but I wonder if much of their discomfort was because they were not accustomed to a 7'2" African American man with an extensive vocabulary and the conviction to convert to Islam, despite his celebrity status and against the will of his parents. I used to tell people that I really liked him because he dominated basketball on every level in which he played. Actually, that was only part of the reason; I also enjoyed watching white reporters be uncomfortable around Abdul-Jabbar but not be in a position to simply dismiss him. There were not too many black people you could say that about in the mid-1970s.

The summer passed quickly and I moved reluctantly to Nashville. My new school was not very different from my old one. It was small, Catholic, and had no more than 10 African American students combined in grades 1 through 8. I was a good student, a fairly conscientious person, and was accustomed to being in the overwhelming racial minority in school, so I adjusted fine. The big test for me was to find out how I stacked up against my peers in the seventh and eighth grades on the basketball court.

As basketball season neared, the seventh and eighth grade boys began to talk about the upcoming season. Unlike me, they almost seemed to dread the fact that football season was ending and basketball was just around the corner. I could not make sense of the situation because it appeared as though most of the guys really enjoyed talking about basketball, and some even looked like they might be pretty good players. Finally I asked, "Why isn't anyone excited about basketball tryouts?" The response I got was, "because Herb Williams coaches the junior high team, and he's really mean." This did not mean very much to me. I had played for alleged "disciplinarian" coaches before with no problem, so I just assumed they were all wimps. A few weeks later, however, I got a taste of what they meant.

When tryouts arrived I was anxious to strut my stuff on the court. I remember walking in the gym with my father earlier than most people. Because it was my first year at the school, my dad wanted to meet the coach. Their meeting was uneventful. My father introduced himself to Herb Williams; they shook hands and exchanged pleasantries. Next Herb turned to me and said, "I sure hope you're a good ballplayer because we sure need it." I remember wondering, "he seems nice enough, why all the fuss from the guys at school?" Within 10 minutes after the tryouts started any fear that I had of not making the team had vanished. We started by dribbling the length of the floor and shooting layups with each hand. More than a handful of the guys could not do it, and this was something that I was quite comfortable and adept at doing. I managed to shine at this and the other drills and was told at the end of the tryout that I had earned a spot on the team. When the team was determined, I was the only African American on it. This was not surprising given that no other blacks even tried out. It felt a bit awkward to me because even though I was used to being either one of a few or the only one in the classroom, the black presence on the basketball teams I had played on was always significant.

After the team had been chosen and real practices started, I began to understand the hesitations about playing for Herb Williams. A fairly large man with a stare that struck fear in you, Herb was unyielding in his criticism and not afraid to explain your weaknesses loud enough for everyone in the gymnasium to hear them. Initially when Herb yelled at me it seemed no different than when he criticized any other player. But soon after I began to really monitor his words, it always came back to me displaying more discipline on the court. I played point guard, which is the position that people often look to as leading and directing the team. Also, much like the quarterback in football, the point guard is considered the person who has to be an extension of the coach on the court or field. The characteristics normally associated with the point guard and quarterback are intelligence, patience, and cool under pressure. These attributes were not associated with black athletes during the late 1970s and early 1980s. Thus black quarterbacks were very unusual at almost every level of football. In the rare instances when African Americans did play the position, it was for one of two of two reasons: the school had no white players who played the position, or a black quarterback with exceptional ability was just too good to deny the job. Even in cases when the latter happened, that player was typically moved to another position once he moved on to the college level; the only exception was if he played at a historically black college or university. As an avid sports fan already, I was aware of the stereotype that blacks were not best suited for the quarterback and point guard positions, so when Coach Williams questioned my discipline on the court I was insulted.

That his insinuations troubled me must have been obvious to Coach Williams, as he pulled me aside after practice to discuss the change in my demeanor. I explained my concern to him, and it was at this point that I realized he was more than an insensitive screamer who only cared about winning the game. He told me that his intention was simply to help me learn and grow as a player. I accepted his explanation, and even thought that perhaps I overreacted. Ultimately I gained a measure of respect for

Coach Williams because of how he handled this situation and assumed that I would have no such thoughts again about my race being a factor on the court.

I had been to predominately white schools long enough to know that race was still an issue in the context of everyday life. Yet I was young enough and, perhaps, still naïve enough to think that sport could be that sacred space that would ultimately eliminate race as a factor in anything that mattered. So when Coach Williams assured me that I was going to lead his team, even as the new guy on the team, I believed him.

As we prepared to open our season in the parochial league, Coach Williams arranged for us to scrimmage some of the local, public junior high teams. This seemed pretty exciting to me, as I was sure that there would be plenty of black guys playing for those teams. Man was I right. As we arrived at the gymnasium for our first scrimmage, it was clear that this was more than a casual practice game for our competition. The stands were full, a section from their school band was in attendance, and you could smell the popcorn from the parking lot. While this caught me off-guard, I was still very excited about playing against the type of guys I had faced on the playgrounds back in my old neighborhood in Louisville, that is, black and talented. Apparently my teammates were less enthusiastic as they all looked like deer staring into headlights when the game started. When the opposing team immediately jumped out to a big lead, Coach Williams called time out to try to calm our guys down and shift the momentum. As we huddled around him, I was sure that Coach Williams would yell at us to try and get us motivated to play better. When he did scream this was no surprise, but what he said has remained with me since. Coach Williams stated, "You guys are acting like you've never been around niggers before. Heck, we've even got one on our team." At that moment all eyes turned to me, including Coach Williams. Feeling as though I had just been hit with a baseball bat, I turned and walked away from the huddle toward the gymnasium exit, ignoring Coach Williams' plea for me to come back. Once out in the lobby I began to sob uncontrollably, surprising even myself that I was so upset. After all, it was not like I had never been called a nigger before, or that I needed for my teammates to be comfortable in a situation where they were in the vast racial minority. But I had gained a measure of respect for Coach Williams by this time and was disappointed in his actions. More important, I was hurt because I had always seen sports as the venue where race was supposed to be minimized.

I had been led to believe that the only color that anyone should pay attention to was the color of the uniform.

Coach Williams and I managed to talk through this situation; I had no doubt that he was genuinely sorry for his poor choice of words in trying to motivate the team. Under his guidance, I, along with my teammates, improved dramatically as basketball players, even managing to win back-to-back parochial league championships. As I moved on to play high school and college basketball, I often thought about Coach Williams and his "tough-love" and traditional approach to the sport. Ironically, he became the measuring stick by which I gauged every other coach I played for, and none of them were able to get the best out of me as did Coach Williams. He and I have remained in touch over the last 25 years, and I continue to apply lessons learned from him on a daily basis.

I am pleased that Coach Williams and I were able to mend our relationship from that incident in 1978, but I doubt that it could have grown like it did had I not read Abdul-Jabbar's Giant Steps during my high school years. As I have indicated, my admiration for Abdul-Jabbar extended beyond his dominance as a basketball player. But perhaps how I benefited most from exposure to Abdul-Jabbar was how he described the hurt he felt when his high school coach at Power Memorial told him he was playing like a nigger. In his reflection of this very unsettling experience, Abdul-Jabbar expressed the pain that came with exposing himself to his coach only to be dismissed by a negative, racial stereotype. Although I could never compare with Abdul-Jabbar on any basketball level, I understood first-hand what it meant for a young, black ballplayer to endure racial humiliation from his white coach. In a bizarre way I took comfort in knowing that I was not alone in this experience, and that it was not beyond even the person who would go on to become professional basketball's all-time leading scorer.

Much to my surprise, even after earning a doctorate in African American history, I continue to struggle with understanding the magnitude of race on American culture, even in the sporting world where most agree that it should not matter. This book is an attempt to make sense of why race still matters in sport and confirms for me that the road the African American athlete travels is indeed a strange one.

ACKNOWLEDGMENTS

Writing this book has challenged me in ways that I never anticipated. When I began this project three years ago, I was teaching in the history department at Rhodes College and, like most junior faculty members, was working in pursuit of tenured status. By the time of publication, I had forfeited my faculty status and moved on to become a senior-level administrator. Although still at Rhodes College, my duties and responsibilities look dramatically different. This professional transition has turned out to be extremely rewarding but not without its challenges. Ironically, I gained strength from past and present African American athletes, many of whom I examine in this book.

But my support has come from nonathletes as well, and I wish to acknowledge them for their role in this journey. First, a special word of appreciation to my parents, Russell and Benny Wigginton, who have always supported my personal and professional goals. I would also like to thank Rhodes College president Bill Troutt, who, in addition to mentoring me professionally, has given me the flexibility to fulfill many of my scholarly pursuits.

I could never name all of the many people who have helped out along the way with words of encouragement and challenges to my assertions. A few at the top of this list include Jeff Williams, Rob Schutt, Melody Richey, Bob Johnson, and Luther Ivory; a particular note of gratitude goes to Marci Hendrix for her work on the index.

I would be remiss if I did not mention two people who passed on long before I even considered writing this book but nonetheless motivated me throughout the process: my grandmother, Mrs. Suella Haralson Wigginton, and my cousin, Kevin Lamont Patterson. From the time I was a young boy until after I graduated from college, "Miss Suella" reminded me that I owed it to myself to reach my potential. Although Kevin was a sickly youth and died too young, I could always rely on the memories of his contagious laugh and lust for life to help keep me plugging away.

Finally, I dedicate *The Strange Career of the Black Athlete* to my wife, Dr. Anita A. Davis, who has been my intellectual inspiration and best friend since we met as college students 20 years ago. I am a better person because of her love, support, and understanding.

FOREWORD

When I was named executive director of the National Association for the Advancement of Colored People (NAACP) in 1977, I declared that under my leadership the organization would stand up and be counted. I made this statement at a time when our organization had limited financial resources and a judgment of a million dollars against it in Mississippi when the hot days of the civil rights movement were cooling off and membership was declining. Despite these conditions, I maintained that the NAACP's work was not complete. In my heart I knew that as long as racial disparities and injustices were visible at every turn, there was still plenty of work to be done. Throughout the next 15 years in the position of executive director, I did my best to motivate African Americans and concerned citizens to work together to right the wrongs they witnessed in employment opportunities, biased laws, insufficient schools, and dilapidated local communities. Hopefully I influenced a few people to keep their foot on the civil rights pedal so that all Americans could enjoy the rights and privileges available to some in our nation.

In that same spirit, *The Strange Career of the Black Athlete* reminds us that the journey toward equality includes all aspects of society—even sports. This nuanced assessment furthers our understanding of the trials and tribulations African American athletes have undergone from the late nineteenth century to the present. An important theme throughout the book is the stifling influence of perpetual racism, regardless of sport, gender, or time period. Yet in so many instances, even if they never reached the pinnacle of their sport, black athletes refused to accept the places assigned to them by society. While some exposed little to the public and concentrated on athletic performance, others used their sport as a stage to highlight the irrationality of prejudice. The NAACP was well aware of these conditions because we had meeting after meeting with three commissioners—David Stern, Pete Rozelle, Peter Uberoff—and the leading Black athletes—Frank Robinson, Joe Black, Hank Aaron, Arthur Ashe—to help eradicate racism.

In reading *The Strange Career of the Black Athlete*, I cannot help but think about how much has changed in the sports world in the past approximately 100 years. No longer are black golfers forbidden from earning their playing cards on the PGA tour nor do universities refuse to play another school because a black player is on the team. Olympic champions are no longer denied the opportunity to dine in the restaurant or lodge in the hotel of their choice once returning home. But I would be remiss if I did not challenge today's African American athlete in the same way that I challenged black America when I took over as executive director of the NAACP almost 30 years ago: Remember those who came before you, and stand up and be counted. There is still plenty of work to do.

Reverend Benjamin L. Hooks
Former Executive Director of the NAACP

1

CAN THEY REALLY PLAY? AFRICAN AMERICAN PARTICIPATION IN "WHITE" SPORTS

In perhaps his most significant written work outside the scholarly masterpiece, *The Souls of Black Folk*, W.E.B. Du Bois challenged all of America to allow the "best" of the Negro race to reach their potential. Du Bois's provocative article, "The Talented Tenth," also published in 1903, stated "The Negro race, like all races, is going to be saved by its exceptional men. The problem of education, then, among Negroes must first of all deal with the Talented Tenth; it is the problem of developing the Best of this race that they may guide the Mass away from contamination and death of the Worst, in their own and other races."[1] Although Du Bois was clearly referring to the responsibilities designated for the shoulders of the black educational elite, his message also pertained to the exceptional athletes who had the courage and conviction to enter into sporting worlds where blacks did not previously have a presence.

Recent scholars have taken more notice of these great athletes and the magnitude of sports in general on America's cultural landscape. Despite this attention to the significance of athletics—past and present—few have looked closely at the sports whose integration attempts did not have lasting results. Specifically, most of the literature focuses on the impact that integration has had on the "big four" sports in twentieth century America: boxing, baseball, basketball, and football. This important work continues to help us appreciate how the complex relationships between racial mores and sports influence our society. Yet it offers little in the way of understanding sports that were dominated by whites as far back as 100 years ago and, in essence, remain the same today.

The phenomenon of certain sports maintaining their whiteness is particularly intriguing when considering the controversial argument accepted by many that African Americans' natural physicality resulting from bone or muscle structure, lung capacity, or the numerous other rationale explains blacks' athletic prowess. Consequently, if one accepts the perspective that African Americans are innately superior on the gridiron, court, diamond, or in the ring, then quite naturally, whites possess an intellectual and academic capacity that exceeds all but the exceptional black person. Hence, when looking at the numerous prominent sports in our society that remain white, the fact remains that the "black equal brawn and white equal wit" perspective held by many does not stand up. Unless, of course, the sports that have been able to maintain their "whiteness" can justify doing so with other, nonphysical explanations. Thus, this chapter examines how some sports have been able to continue their dominant white presence over the years.

I focus here on horse racing, golf, hockey, and tennis. Each of these sports has experienced integration attempts by African American pioneers, but their efforts have not had a sustainable impact on the racial demography of the sport today. To answer why this has been the case, I will consider questions such as these: What characteristics have defined "whiteness" in American society and these particular sports? What was the broader historical context in which black athletes entered the sport? How did the entrance or exit of blacks in these sports influence public perceptions?

Since the earliest encounters of Atlantic nations of Europe with Africa during the sixteenth century, the marked contrast in color of Africans influenced European perceptions. The darker skin color of Africans compared to Europeans, which came to be described in the exaggerated term *black*, carried with it several negative connotations that became the ingredients of racially based prejudice and racism. In other words, the Africans' color set them apart, and Europeans needed ways to make sense of the difference. They found multiple explanations. Initially, the African's appearance (including color, wool-like hair, and other physical distinctions) was thought to be a physical one caused by their exposure to the sun. This answer alone was not deemed satisfactory, so other reasons were considered. Europeans observed the African religious and cultural practices that were unlike their own, and they began to question if Africans' skin color was the result of other flaws. Hence the notion of an internal blackness, perhaps caused by heathenism or a curse, became a viable explanation. In all, the manner by which Europeans measured Africans, that is, through European lenses, became the foundation for a culture of white superiority that has since dominated American culture.[2]

As America was finding its place in the world in the seventeenth century, the need for labor and the moral and physical rationalizations of Africans as an available supply created a system of racial-based slavery. Slavery was firmly entrenched into the fabric of society by the mid-seventeenth century, and served as a constant reminder that the white race was superior to the black race. It was this ability to literally own a people that reinforced whites' capacity to dictate the direction of American culture. The justifications of slavery and the subsequent belief that whites were inherently superior to their black counterparts permitted a cultural context in which whites were preoccupied with maintaining their higher status in society. Ultimately, as noted historian U. B. Phillips wrote about the South but was applicable to the entire United States, "the determination to preserve a white man's country was the central theme of southern history."[3]

The complete governance of American society enabled whites to establish and control the values by which people would be measured; those defined as intelligent, hard-working, and ethical were determined by white interpretations without consideration of blacks' merit. The development of labor and work culture in eighteenth-century America reflects what was happening in all of society. Specifically, as historian David Roediger explains, white workers, regardless of skill-level or the indignity of their work, maintained a "wage of whiteness" over all black workers. This meant that even the lowest paid white worker could take solace in the fact that race afforded him access to a privileged world unfamiliar to blacks. This advantage combined with the limited opportunities of even the most talented African American workers ensured that they would always fall short of the white benchmark.[4]

By the 1880s and 1890s, America's commitment to white supremacy was standard practice. Despite occasional examples of their merit, it was common to divide African Americans from whites along social, political, and economic lines. The practice of segregation was validated by law in 1896 with the U.S. Supreme Court decision in *Plessy v. Ferguson*. The

Court ruled that maintaining a separate public sphere was constitutional as long as equal accommodations were provided for blacks.

The ability to control the social, political, and economic rules of a society left no doubt for whites that they were entitled to rule the athletic arena as well. Yet as Du Bois's profound writings of the late nineteenth and early twentieth centuries reveal, by the end of the nineteenth century, African Americans had developed a "double consciousness" that allowed them to maintain a world void of white assessment and rules. And it would be in their black sphere that blacks would nurture their own foundations for racial self-help.

The African American path breakers in horse racing and golf would challenge their legitimacy in the white sporting world during the late nineteenth century. Perhaps like their foremothers and fathers, they rejected the belief system that mental, physical, and moral deficiencies were inherent by-products of being African American. Du Bois's "Talented Tenth" article appeared a few years after a black entered these sports, but his written outcry for justice and equality for all in America was fueled by the racial backlash that dominated the post-Reconstruction era to the end of the nineteenth century.

HORSE RACING

The role of race in American society has been an ongoing experiment since the arrival of the first African slaves in 1619. All one needs to do is look at the voluminous literature that analyzes the fascinating tensions between the legal statutes and social practices from the mid-seventeenth century onward. For example, how does one explain how a state such as South Carolina, in many ways the bastion of slavery in the eighteenth and nineteenth centuries, maintained a culture that also allowed a significant skilled, free black population? It was such a society, filled with contradictions and inconsistencies, that witnessed black prominence in horse racing during the era of slavery. Horse racing allocated space for all to witness—white and black, men and women, aristocracy and peasant, free and enslaved. And it was this smorgasbord of people that lead to horse racing's title of "America's First National Sport."

Best chronicled in his thorough and insightful study, *The Great Black Jockeys*, horse racing scholar Edward Hotaling describes how southern blacks in the colonial and antebellum eras capitalized on their lowly status as slaves or disregarded free laborers to become leading trainers, grooms-men, and jockeys. He describes how the unattractive, arduous labor asso-ciated with maintaining horses usually meant that it was passed on to black workers. Thus performing the undesirable duties, typically referred to as "nigger work," gave blacks an important presence in what quickly became an American pastime. By the beginning of the nineteenth cen-tury, this involvement led to the majority of jockeys in the South being black slaves who were quite familiar with horses and the horsing industry.[5]

Slave jockeys continued their prominence and dominance throughout the first half of the nineteenth century, even as the nation became preoc-cupied with the events of the Civil War. As Hotaling notes, "just after the infamous battle of African American soldiers of the fifty-forth regiment at Fort Wagner, South Carolina in August 1863, racing fans at the newly minted Saratoga, New York track witnessed the ride to victory by a one-eyed, escaped slave known only as Sewell."[6] In many ways, the coinci-dence of Sewell's victory on the heels of the representation of the black fighting spirit challenged the persona that whites had rationalized for many years, at least in the sporting world. As emancipation was granted and the Civil War came to and end, it would be impossible to think of black jockeys as merely talented horse riders without recognizing that they were competitive and determined men as well.

The false dichotomy of chattel slave versus human being that domi-nated American antebellum life, and the threatening implications of establishing the racial rules that would preoccupy much of the nation dur-ing the immediate postwar years, would also symbolize the changing role of African Americans in horse racing. The magnitude of horse racing in American life would continue to soar, and those connected to the sport would begin to take steps to redefine the presence and significance of black jockeys in the sport.

The year 1875 symbolized the beginnings of the intimate connection between racial mores in the postwar period and how these decisions influ-enced the racial demographic of horse racing. In that year, Congress passed a Civil Rights Act that forbade discrimination in public spaces such as hotels and trains. Of interest, 1875 was also the year that the Kentucky Derby was born. In anticipation of the great national spectacle that it would become, the *Louisville Courier-Journal* said on its inaugural race day, "Today will be historic for Kentucky annals as the first 'Derby Day' of what promises to be a long series of annual festivities, which we confidently expect our grandchildren a hundred years hence to celebrate in glorious centennial rejoicings."[7]

The country's obsession with horse racing, combined with the promise of the Kentucky Derby as the premier race in the country, meant that society played close attention to the outcome of the "Running of the Roses." That the winning horse was Aristedes was not a surprise, as he was one of the favorites of the race. Nor was it attention-worthy that the jockey atop Aristedes was African American rider Oliver Lewis. The most striking aspect of this first Derby was that a black jockey was almost predetermined to cross the finish line first, as 14 of the 15 riders in the race were African American. This by itself was not cause for alarm for the horse racing industry, but when reviewing the race's history for the remainder of the nineteenth century, black jockeys took home the top prize 12 more times.[8]

The most noted of the African American jockeys to win the Kentucky Derby was Isaac Murphy. Murphy won this prestigious race three times, becoming the first jockey of any color to achieve this feat. Murphy's success in the Kentucky Derby and other prominent races of his day earned him the label of the greatest African American athlete of the nineteenth century. His exceptional riding abilities led the well-known Murphy to be the most desirable jockey that a horse owner could attract. As a result, Murphy had the opportunity to mount the most recognized horses of his era. His talents combined with riding the best horses helped Murphy amass a remarkable winning rate of 44 percent. But the most amazing aspect of Murphy's chronicled career may not be the successes he enjoyed as a rider. Rather, it is the fascinating story of how this great African American jockey's career coincided with society's conscious demise of black presence in sports and the country.

Most scholars agree that Civil Rights Act of 1875 was only a "courtesy act" that had little bearing on the racial practices of the day. Yet symbolically, this act gave African Americans hope that they might successfully move toward real equity in society. In 1883, this dream of racial equality was dismissed as the U.S. Supreme Court ruled that the Civil Rights Act of 1875 was unconstitutional, making it official that society was reluctant to use the government as a monitor for people's social practices. The Court's decision was an early indicator of the national trend to harden the lines of racial segregation throughout the country. Just as important, it signaled that northern involvement in southern racial practices was diminishing.

It is ironic that Murphy began his professional riding year in Louisville in 1875, but not at the famed Kentucky Derby. Although Murphy did not finish in the money in his first race, it would not be long before he would become the premier rider of his era. As Murphy began winning races and his dominance became acknowledged nationally, his reputation and status as a top jockey began to undergo a transformation from that of a rider of tremendous skill and integrity, to a jockey who lacked discipline and practiced haughty showmanship. Murphy's reputation as a "hand rider"— a rider who rarely needed to use the whip, and the grace and ease in which he seemed to control his mount was the envy of the profession. And, his reluctance to place bets or have bets placed for him on races was unusual, as jockeys were notorious for betting against themselves and subsequently losing races on purpose during the 1880s and 1890s.[9]

At the same time, Murphy's riding record and prestige brought about increased earnings believed to be three or four times that of the other top jockeys of his day. This type of income discrepancy allowed Murphy to enjoy a much publicized life of leisure, which distinguished him even further from his fellow riders. One example specific to Kentucky was Murphy's financial ability to purchase a home in an exclusive white neighborhood. Murphy broke no laws by living here, but his presence in this Lexington community came at a time when white citizens were beginning to pressure public officials to create mechanisms for this to cease; only a few years later and a short piece down the road in Louisville, a residential segregation ordinance was implemented to keep this from happening. Louisville's efforts to designate certain sections of town as white and others as black would culminate in the fierce legal battle of *Buchanan v. Warley* (1917), fought at the U.S. Supreme Court. Ultimately the Court determined that residential segregation along racial lines was unconstitutional, but the fact that such a case was initiated in the city of Louisville reinforces the intensity and dominance of Jim Crow laws, even in a region of the country considered "race friendly."

Murphy's attributes would probably have caused problems for any jockey during the late nineteenth century, but the racial climate of the day ensured criticism at best and rejection at worst for any black jockey. The methodical legal changes initiated in the 1880s ensured that the races would maintain separate public and social space. By the 1890s, these laws validated the already acceptable practices of segregation. These restrictive rules in society followed a similar pattern in the sporting world, making it easier to eliminate or, at a minimum, reduce significantly the presence of blacks in athletics. He no longer dominated the premier races, and antagonists began to criticize him for an alleged drinking problem and lack of commitment to the sport. Murphy's impeccable reputation as a skilled and ethical rider was under scrutiny. Some even questioned whether or not he had succumbed to throwing races. Murphy was out of racing completely by the early 1890s. He died of pneumonia prematurely in 1896. Most agree that Murphy was susceptible to this illness because of his excessive drinking and the unhealthy dietary habits required for maintaining his riding weight over the years. Because of his status as the best jockey of the era, Murphy's rapid decline in the early 1890s probably contributed more to the demise of African American jockeys than any other black rider in history.

The success of Murphy and the other top black jockeys of the day combined with the more lucrative economic rewards spurred white jockeys and the horse racing industry to find ways to distinguish themselves from their black counterparts. The most effective way that they found to accomplish this was the establishment of the Jockey Club. Started in 1894, this association began widespread efforts to control all aspects of horse racing, including the power to limit the number of licensed black jockeys in the sport. The industry's recognition of jockey unions symbolized, in effect, the beginning of the end of the black jockey's presence in the sport.

Of interest, the Jockey Club's emphasis and subsequent strength was primarily in the northeastern region of the country. As Hotaling suggests, much of horse racing's big money and prestige had shifted to the Northeast where most of the large stable owners were located. This shift coincided with the first wave of a series of black migration efforts from the South to the North. Between 1880 and the turn of the century, cities such as Philadelphia, New York, Washington, and Chicago experienced major demographic changes with the arrival of black southerners looking to escape the South's racial constraints. For the first time, white northerners were faced with a longtime reality of southern life—sharing society with African Americans. Like most white southerners, white northerners responded with de facto and de jure methods to distance themselves from their new "neighbors." In essence, the same threats and pressures that black residents presented to the status quo in northern society contributed to the Jockey Club's decision to gradually deny black riders licensure as a way to eliminate them from the sport.[10]

A few African American jockeys managed to have some success in horse racing's big stake races in the final years of the nineteenth century and into the early years of the twentieth (Jimmy Winkfield won the Kentucky Derby in 1902 and Jimmy Lee the Travers at Saratoga in 1908), but most faced insurmountable obstacles in the United States and were forced to take their talents to Russia or other European countries to make a decent living. As these discouraged jockeys fled the horse racing scene in America, there were not many African American riders in the pipeline to replace them. And for those who attempted to carry on this rich legacy of riding excellence, few could even get a decent horse to mount. Most owners were afraid to risk hiring a black jockey for fear that white riders would work together to ensure that a black jockey would not win a race, regardless of the quality of the horse. This lack of opportunity meant a rapid decline of black jockeys in the 1920s and 1930s. By the end of the 1930s less than 15 of approximately 950 licensed jockeys were African American. This trend continued, and by the mid-1970s, no more than 10 black riders were listed out of more than 1,000 American jockeys. Unfortunately, the void of African Americans in horse racing today has left many to think of black jockeys only as "lawn jockeys" rather than the elite and desirous status they once held.

GOLF

Many scholars date the involvement of African Americans in golf back to the early days of the sport's arrival to the United States in the late eighteenth century. Yet perceptions of their roles in the game are typically relegated to caddying or some other type of subservient position. This is not surprising when considering the country's commitment to racial-based slavery or, at least, social segregation along racial lines. Golfing was identified as a game to be enjoyed by an exclusive few. Yet much like African Americans did in all aspects of America's emerging culture, they contributed to and bore some of the fruits of this new game.

Numerous black individuals contributed to golf's development over the years, but as is often the case, too few received official acknowledgment by their contemporaries. Dr. George Grant and John Shippen fall into this category. Grant built his reputation as an outstanding dentist after becoming the first African American to graduate from Harvard Dental School in 1870. He was respected enough to be invited back as a member of the faculty four years later. Grant was known to be an avid golfer as early as the 1880s, but his most important contribution to golf was inventing the golf tee. Grant's wonderful improvement for the game was granted patent 638,920 by the U.S. Patent Office in 1899. Grant died in 1910 and, unfortunately, he had never exposed his invention to the general public. Ironically, another dentist, Dr. William Lowell, reinvented the tee a decade later. Unlike Grant, Lowell marketed the idea to the public. This convenient tool for golfers was a popular item, and, by 1925, there were several brands of tees for golfers to enjoy. Because of the tee's popularity after Lowell's reintroduction, he was given credit for inventing this item that quickly became a necessity for golfers of all levels. Finally, in 1991, after much determination by an African American professor, Grant was acknowledged as the real inventor of the tee by the United States Golf Association (USGA).[11]

John Shippen was probably the most prominent African American golfer to be denied his proper place in the sport's history. In 1896, at the young age of 16, Shippen became the first American-born and African American, professional golfer. Shippen, along with Native American golfer, Oscar Bunn, decided to enter the USGA-sponsored U.S. Open Championship at the new Shinnecock Hills Golf Club that year. Shippen and Bunn had both worked in the building of the course, and had been taught some of the finer points of the game by club owner Willie Dunn. Shippen's ability caught the eye of club members, and they encouraged him and Bunn to enter the tournament. Once the professional entrants heard about Shippen and Bunn's plans to play, they threatened to boycott participation in the championship. Although most professional golfers during this era were not American-born, they obviously shared typical American attitudes about race. Indeed, 1896 was the year that separation by race would become legal in the U.S. Supreme Court case of *Plessy v. Ferguson*.

Surprisingly, USGA president Theodore Havemeyer stood firm to the challenge and announced that the tournament would proceed as scheduled, even if Shippen and Bunn were the only two golfers on the course. Havemeyer was reported to have diffused the situation by claiming that Shippen was only "half black," with his other half being of Indian descent.

Nevertheless, proclaiming that Shippen and Bunn would be allowed to play at all costs was a bold and unusual move in the late nineteenth century. Perhaps Havemeyer considered the irony in the situation. This was indeed the U.S. Open, and Shippen and Bunn were technically more "American" than most of the protesting golfers. The tournament took place without incident, and Shippen performed admirably. He shot an impressive 78 in the first round, which tied him with four other players for first place. In the second and final round, Shippen struggled a bit and shot an 81. Still, he finished tied for fifth place and earned $10 for his performance. Shippen participated in four more U.S. Open championships, never finishing better than fifth place.[12]

Despite the dual accomplishments of being the first African American and American-born professional golfer, Shippen's legacy remained virtually unknown to even the most devoted golfers and sports fanatics until 1995. That year the John Shippen Memorial Golf Foundation was founded, giving this great golf pioneer the recognition that he so richly deserved. To finally acknowledge Shippen's contributions was a significant step for the annals of golf, but doing so almost a full century later draws attention to two major questions: What took so long? Why then? The answers are a combination of the commitment by whites to maintain some "racial space," an unyielding desire by blacks to attain equal access to the game and the emergence of Tiger Woods on the Professional Golfers' Association tour. How these two responses intersect is reflected in the experiences of African American golfing firsts in the context of race relations in the twentieth century.

The inaugural U.S. Open in 1895, the year before Shippen and Bunn entered the tournament, symbolized America's growing enthusiasm for golf. Increased interest worked hand-in-glove with expanding the number of public, municipal courses, especially in the northeastern and midwestern regions of the country. Golf had also recently founded the United States Golf Association (1894) to establish the rules and act as a governing body for the sport. These initiatives did note erase golf's elitist and exclusive reputation entirely, but it did expose the game to a wider audience. African Americans, along with the approximately 500,000 immigrants the country accepted each year, were a significant part of this constituency.

The outbreak of World War I in 1914 reduced immigration to a trickle. This group, however, was replaced by an unprecedented number of

African American migrants from the South to the North. Recognized as the Great Migration, approximately 500,000 black southerners arrived in northern and midwestern cities from 1915 to 1918. They were followed by at least 700,000 more in the 1920s. This major demographic shift may be attributed to a combination of "push-and-pull" factors. The combination of sharecropping work, economic hardships, and stifling racism was easy for many black southerners to leave, especially with the promises of economic prosperity and better housing and educational opportunities waiting in the North.

Without question, the influx of African Americans to cities such as Chicago, Detroit, Cleveland, Philadelphia, and New York changed the social, political, and economic landscape in each place. Throughout the North, battle lines for jobs, housing, and schools were drawn between blacks and whites. One series of examples occurred in Chicago and their severe housing problems. Immediately after the U.S. Supreme Court decision in *Buchanan v. Warley* (1917), the Chicago Real Estate Board promoted the need for property owners' associations in an effort to keep neighborhoods white. This initiative contributed to the eventual race riot throughout the entire city in 1919.[13]

The theme of maintaining whiteness was also at the forefront of the golfing world. In 1916, a group of wealthy white men formed the Professional Golfers' Association of America (PGA) to join forces with the USGA as the governing bodies of amateur and professional golf in America. Although neither group had written laws specific to race at this time, it was commonplace for African Americans to be rejected from PGA- or USGA-sponsored events.[14]

Given the context of racial violence and unrest in Chicago, it is not surprising that some of the first noted challenges to segregated golf took place in that city. At least two of these challenges were led by Walter Speedy. Like many other blacks, Speedy had arrived in Chicago from the South during the mass migration. On his arrival, Speedy pursued legal action for the opportunity to play in Chicago's public course tournaments. His most intense confrontation occurred with the Chicago Parks Department in 1921. Speedy and a few other African American golfers had registered to play in a public tournament, but their names had been erased and replaced with those of two white golfers. The black golfers attempted to take legal action, but they were denied an injunction on a technicality. Speedy and the other black golfers' attempts to play in Chicago's public tournaments were unsuccessful, but they did bring attention to the issue of race in the sport of golf. By doing so, they helped galvanize aspiring African American, professional golfers around the country to do what blacks had done in other aspects of their lives; they created their own organization.[15]

After years of regional black-specific organizations, the United States Colored Golf Association became the first national black golf association in 1925. The group, which changed its name to the United Golfers Association (UGA) after a few years, became the backbone for African American golfers. In its early years the UGA served as the organizing body for black professional tournaments. At the same time, the UGA worked relentlessly to encourage the PGA to take down its exclusionary practices. By the late 1950s, the UGA was seen in the same light as the Negro leagues in baseball, as a minor league for the PGA to hand-pick the African American golfers it would allow on the PGA tour. Yet the battles that the UGA and black golfers would fight until the late 1950s to early 1960s would be long, arduous fights.

The USGA and PGA seemed to maintain business as usual until Dewey Brown became the first African American golfer allowed to join the PGA in 1928. Many believe that Brown's membership was merely a glitch in PGA practices, claiming that his fair skin may have been mistaken for white. This explanation seems very possible, especially when considering that Brown's membership was revoked in 1934 without cause.[16] In 1943, the PGA made its position on race very clear by inserting a "Caucasian clause" into its constitution. Although a major setback for aspiring black professional golfers, this formal policy at least gave them a direct target to attack. Like the strategy used to combat racial justice in many other segments of American society, African American golfers focused on the legal system.

The most recognized legal battle that spurred the PGA to address its discriminatory was a lawsuit filed by black professionals Bill Spiller, Teddy Rhodes, and Madison Gunther on January 17, 1948. Their claim was based on the fact that each had qualified for a professional tournament in which they had been denied entry. The lawsuit was dropped after the PGA proposed to stop their discriminatory practices. The PGA reneged on its promise and used creative loopholes to maintain the status quo. Still, the 1948 lawsuit rejuvenated the efforts to give black professional golfers access to the PGA tour. Eventually the sustained pressure to integrate the PGA tour paid off when Charles Sifford was granted PGA membership in 1960. In November of the next year, the infamous "Caucasian clause" was removed from the PGA by-laws.[17]

Sifford's membership represented more than 60 years of struggle for African American golfers' fight for equal treatment. His momentous achievement was cause for celebration, but everyone knew that in many ways it was the beginning rather than the culmination. Sifford was joined in the 1960s by pioneers such as Pete Brown, the first black to win a PGA tournament, and Lee Elder, the first black to play in the Masters, but the entry of African Americans on the PGA tour has continued to happen at a snail's pace for the last 40 years.

Golf continues to have a reputation of exclusivity reserved for the white and wealthy. Admittedly the game has increased in popularity beyond the elite, but not to the degree that it takes to produce significant diversity at the professional level. It remains an extremely expensive and time-consuming sport—two resources unavailable to most people, especially African Americans. Even the minimum requirements include clubs, a place to practice, and coaching. For PGA members, this has usually meant being introduced to the game at a very young age, clubs appropriate for their age and size, membership at a country club, and access to the club professional or other premier teachers of the game. When considering this list, the overwhelming majority of people are eliminated from competing at the top level, even if they display an aptitude for the game early on.

Undoubtedly, Tiger Woods turning professional and joining the PGA tour in 1996 has expanded interest in the sport, not only for African Americans, but the "average" man or woman. For example, it is hard to image that his presence on the golf scene and playing in the centennial U.S. Open at Shinnecock Hills in 1995 was not the impetus for creating the John Shippen Memorial Golf Foundation. Further, the dramatic increase in golf's television viewers, the demographic diversity of the spectators who now attend professional tournaments and the explosion of play on local public courses are evidence that the sport has a new and captive audience.

Golf has certainly benefited financially by its expanded pool of people interested in the sport, but for African Americans in particular, this has not resulted in a greater presence on the PGA tour. The sport should be credited for several initiatives to be more inclusive in the last 10 to 15 years, but the question remains: Is enough being done? It is imperative that the PGA continue to implement innovative and, perhaps, expensive programs to capitalize on their opportunity to make golf a truly inclusive game. In other words, as the "I Am Tiger Woods" Nike commercial suggests, let's find out if there are really some more Tiger Woods out there to take the game to an even higher level. The consequences of not doing so might mean that Woods's legacy will be that he was an exceptional golfer not because of his tremendous playing ability, but because he was a black player in an extremely white game.

HOCKEY

Hockey's introduction to the United States was by way of Canada. Although the official beginning of the sport is disputed by hockey buffs, leading hockey scholar, Brian McFarlane, traces the game back to the British Royal Family in the 1850s. According to McFarlane, the game crossed the Atlantic Ocean to Canada in the late nineteenth century and, by the 1890s, was clearly a passion for the country. In 1893, Canadian governor general Lord Stanley of Preston began a tradition that still stands as the ultimate in the hockey world. Stanley awarded a silver bowl, referred to as the Stanley Cup, to the best Canadian hockey team of the year. Now, the cup goes to the team recognized as the best in the National Hockey League (NHL).[18]

The popularity of hockey in Canada led to the development of professional hockey leagues throughout the country with the NHL as the top league. Much like baseball has done with its professional minor leagues in this country, those worthy of professional status but who have not reached the sports highest league played in leagues of different skill levels. The enthusiasm for the game slowly trickled down to the United States, and, in 1924, an NHL franchise was awarded to the city of Boston. Other American cities were gradually awarded teams, but it remained very much a sport for northern and eastern locations with weather more conducive to the sport.

Despite its mostly regional status, hockey continued to gain in popularity in the United States over the next several decades. A vivid indication that this sport had gained significant interest was the decision to broadcast NHL games on television for the first time during the 1956–57 hockey season. The sports introduction to a national audience was certainly not considered a threat to "America's pastime" of baseball, but the context of hockey's growth in America, especially when looking at the experiences of black pioneers trying to break the color barrier in both sports, offers some intriguing linkages usually not considered.

The story of Jackie Robinson's entrance into and influence on major league baseball is well chronicled. Robinson represented not only an unprecedented hope for black participation in sports, but also symbolized a spirit in America that maybe, just maybe, African Americans would have equal access to all that the country had to offer. His presence in the beloved game of baseball in 1947, a game that much of white America felt they "owned," made the countless efforts and multiple strategies of blacks searching for equality throughout the years seem worthwhile. African Americans attributed the crashing of the seemingly insurmountable racist wall of baseball segregation to their patriotic sentiment, bold activism, and heroic military accomplishments during the World War II era. In particular, a survey of blacks revealed that approximately two-thirds felt that they had a major stake in the war's outcome and more than 40 percent believed that the race conditions in America would improve after the war. Also, the infamous threat by the March on Washington Movement to protest the nation's segregated military and exclusionary hiring practices in government jobs sent the message again that African Americans had to be reckoned with. This challenge was initiated by longtime civil and labor rights activist, A. Philip Randolph, who informed President Franklin Delano Roosevelt that he, Randolph, would lead 100,000 blacks on a protest march on the nation's capital. Such a bold move was unusual in 1941, but President Roosevelt took it seriously and issued Executive Order #8802 as a first step to investigate incidents of employment discrimination. These dynamics combined with the nation's acknowledgment of its black soldiers' role in victory set the foundation for what many hoped would be a new way of life.

During the same time that Jackie Robinson was matriculating through the Los Angeles Dodgers organization on his way to integrating baseball's major leagues, a comparable effort was in process in Canada's primary sport of hockey. The man recognized as the best candidate to integrate the sport was Herb Carnegie. A native Canadian, Carnegie was born in Toronto in 1919 to George Nathaniel Carnegie and Adina Janes Mitchell. Herb's parents had immigrated from Jamaica to Toronto in 1912, where they would raise their family. Herb grew up in a culture that lacked much of the virulent and in-your-face racial discrimination that was common in the United States at the time, but Canadian society made it clear that "coloured" people were to stay in their place, that is, at the bottom of Canada's social hierarchy.[19]

Carnegie did not allow society's racial restrictions to forfeit his dreams of playing professional hockey at the NHL level. He began his professional career in 1937 as a 17-year-old and got the unique opportunity to play professionally with his brother, Ossie, beginning in the 1940–41 season. Herb and Ossie were standout performers, and in the 1941–42 season they were joined by another black player, Manny McIntyre, to form the first recorded all-black front line in hockey history. The three talented forwards were standout performers together for about five years, with Herb recognized as having the best opportunity to perhaps advance to the top level of the NHL. Herb continued to excel, and in 1947, the same year that Robinson integrated major league baseball in the United States, Carnegie was named team captain for a team in one of the premier minor leagues.[20]

Carnegie won the team's most valuable player award for the 1947 season. After Robinson's monumental achievement of breaking the color barrier in baseball, Carnegie figured this was his best position to date to challenge for a roster slot for an NHL team. His dreams for an opportunity at making an NHL team came true when he received an invitation to the New York Rangers training camp for the 1948 season. By this time Carnegie had completed 10 seasons and had proven himself an exceptional talent in minor league professional hockey. He was also 29 years old in a sport where many careers were winding down, so he realized that this might be his first and last chance at an NHL career. Carnegie had an excellent showing in the camp and had no reason to believe that he had not earned a spot on the Rangers' roster. Despite displaying the skills of an NHL-caliber player, Carnegie was only offered a job on the Rangers top minor league team. Carnegie was told by Frank Boucher, the manager of the Rangers' team, that "you're an excellent hockey player, but I'd like to make sure by sending you first to New Haven."[21] Boucher's words of "I'd like to make sure" have haunted Carnegie since, not because he questioned whether he was good enough to play at hockey's top level, but because it became evident that his race and the sport's unwillingness to accept a black player still superseded ability.

Herb Carnegie rejected Boucher's offer to play for the Rangers minor league affiliate and returned to his most recent team in Sherbrooke. But it was probably at this moment of rejection that Carnegie began to believe what many had told him throughout his young life: even the most talented and hard working people of color could only reach heights that society designated for them. Struck with this reality, Carnegie even allowed himself to believe the statement reportedly expressed years ago by Toronto Maple Leafs' legendary coach, Conn Symthe, who after watching Carnegie play as a junior said, "I'll pay $10,000 to any man that could turn Carnegie white."[22] Carnegie would never forget the sting of racism as his dream of playing in the NHL vanished in one moment. He later said in his autobiography, A Fly in a Pail of Milk, "My dream was unfulfilled and it hurt—that pain has never left me."[23]

The dashed dreams and subsequent broken heart of Carnegie and numerous other black NHL hopefuls would persist for another decade. It was not until January 18, 1958, that Willie O'Ree became the National Hockey League's "Jackie Robinson" when he made his debut with the Boston Bruins. In many ways, O'Ree's hockey career mirrored that of his predecessor Carnegie; both were Canadian natives who became captivated by the sport of hockey like so many other boys in that country; both spent little time focusing on the fact that they were usually the only colored players on their various hockey teams; and both played for the Quebec Aces, noted as one of Canada's elite minor league professional teams. The major difference was that O'Ree got the opportunity to play in the National Hockey League, but, unfortunately, Carnegie never was given that option.

O'Ree's career developed like most any professional hockey player. He fell in love with the sport and began playing in organized and competitive leagues at an early age. Born in Fredericton, New Brunswick in 1935, O'Ree was skating at age three and competing in a league at age five. O'Ree claims that by age 13 he knew that he wanted to play professionally and that "I was obsessed by the game."[24] As he got older, O'Ree's obsession and ability allowed him to play for some of the top junior league teams, which are equivalent to college-level hockey in the United States. During the 1955–56 season, O'Ree suffered a severe injury when he was struck in the right eye by a flying puck. This injury caused him to permanently lose 95 percent of vision in the eye, which would have spelled the end of a promising career to most any other player. Miraculously, O'Ree was able to continue his great play, and turned professional the next season. He spent the 1956–57 season with the Quebec Aces, a minor league affiliate of the Boston Bruins, and impressed enough people that he got his NHL chance during the 1957–58 season. O'Ree played in only two games that season, and spent the next few years back in the minor leagues until the Bruins recalled him during the 1960–61 season. This time O'Ree's stay was longer, playing in 43 games. That O'Ree stayed with the Bruins for over half a season suggested that he had finally made it to the NHL, especially since after the 1961 season, the Bruins' general manager, Lynn Patrick, told him "Go home and have a good summer. We're impressed with your play. You'll be back with the Bruins."[25] O'Ree went home to Fredericton enthusiastic about his chances the next season, only to find out from a reporter that he had been traded to the talent-laden Montreal Canadians. Never being contacted by the Bruins and the depth of the Canadians' team gave O'Ree cause for concern about his hockey career. His inclination was right and, despite playing professionally for 17 more seasons, O'Ree would never skate on NHL ice after 1961.[26]

O'Ree never understood why he never returned to hockey's major leagues; he had proven that he had the talent, skill, and work ethic; no major racial incidents occurred in more than 40 games, and he seemingly handled the slurs and epithets with dignity. Years after his career ended, why he was relegated to the minor leagues after 1961 remained a mystery to O'Ree. Two other important questions related to O'Ree remain unanswered: Why was there virtually no fanfare about his breaking the color barrier in 1958? And why has the presence of African Americans in the NHL remained almost nonexistent more than 40 years later?

When asked his reaction to the media barely mentioning his appearance in the NHL in 1958, O'Ree replied, "It really didn't matter to me. I was too excited about beating the Canadians in the Forum. I was just a kid trying to make a team."[27] Certainly, O'Ree had to keep focused on his goal of proving that he could compete at hockey's top competition level, but one can hardly imagine that he did not recognize the significance of the first time that his skates hit the ice in a Bruins uniform. The standard responses for the lack of acknowledgment for O'Ree's accomplishments are that hockey's home country was Canada and not the United States, and that Canada did not experience the same degree of racial discrimination that haunted American history. Admittedly, there is some truth to this rationale. If America had the same passion about hockey that they exuded for baseball in 1958, O'Ree would have likely reached icon status like Jackie Robinson. And, without the legacy of slavery, Jim Crow laws, and significant black population, Canadians were not preoccupied with race as was the case in the United States.

But it is precisely this turbulent history of racial prejudice in the United States that makes the lack of attention paid to O'Ree's presence in the NHL startling, especially when considering the context of race relations during the late 1950s and early 1960s when he cracked the color line. From 1950–60, America experienced unprecedented legal, political, and social challenges to the racial status quo. This period, the first of two decades recognized as the Civil Rights Movement, witnessed path-breaking initiatives such as the *Brown v. Board of Education* decision. This legal act against segregation, along with numerous others, took important steps toward correcting society's racial inequalities.

The landmark *Brown v. Board of Education* decision, handed down by the U.S. Supreme Court on May 17, 1954, is considered by many to be the anchor for African Americans achieving equity in the twentieth century. After more than 20 years of race and education court cases leading up to this one, the verdict in *Brown* eliminated the "separate but equal" doctrine that had reinforced white supremacy since the late nineteenth century. The celebration surrounding equal rights by law was short-lived, however, as the majority of white Americans were unwilling to relinquish their culture of superiority because the law had changed. The result was an intense backlash aimed at maintaining white control at all costs. Ranging from the organized efforts of the White Citizens' Councils and the Southern Manifesto, to extralegal actions such as physical threats and violence, it was soon evident that society would not transform quickly or easily.

The context of race relations in Boston from 1950–60 also plays an important role in explaining O'Ree's limited exposure. Boston's history of race relations is complex and, at times, contradictory. From as far back as the colonial period, Bostonians debated about the "status of the Negro" in their city. At times it appeared that Boston was a leader in providing opportunities for its black citizens; yet on other occasions the city fought relentlessly to uphold racial discrimination. Such discrepancy was usually about the degree of equality "by law" and "by practice" that blacks should
l. Perhaps the racial dynamic of Boston was captured best by century Boston mayor, Harrison Gray Otis, who in 1831 oston's black citizens as "a quiet, inoffensive, and in many eful race, but the repugnance to intimate social relations with

them is insurmountable."[28] In many ways, Otis's words captured the designated place for black Bostonians even in the twentieth century.

Racial integration in Boston's professional sports, particularly in basketball and baseball, followed the same contradictory patterns found in the
city's overall history. For example, the city's professional basketball team,
the Boston Celtics, was the first team in the National Basketball Association to draft an African American player when they chose Chuck Cooper
of Duquesne University in 1950. Reportedly, when Celtics owner Walter
Brown chose Cooper, he was questioned by another owner for picking a
black player. Brown replied, "I don't give a damn if he's striped or plaid or
polka dot, Boston takes Charles Cooper of Duquesne."[29]

The integration of major league baseball in Boston, however, would be
much more reflective of the city's complex relationship with African
Americans. First, at the time that Jackie Robinson integrated major league
baseball in 1947, Boston still had two major league teams, the Boston
Braves and Boston Red Sox. Ironically, each team had an opportunity to
sign Jackie Robinson in 1945 when he and two other stars from the Negro
leagues earned tryouts. Unfortunately, it was evident from the beginning
that neither team was serious about leading the effort to integrate baseball.
The Red Sox granted them tryouts. Despite impressing the team's coaches,
the players were told only that the team would be in touch. The phone call
or letter never came for any of the players. The Braves, on the other hand,
backed out of their agreement to give the players a look and never showed
up to evaluate the players. Of course Robinson went on to sign with the
Brooklyn Dodgers that year and worked his way up to the major leagues
two years later. Surprisingly, the Boston Braves signed black outfielder
Sam Jethroe in 1950, making them only the fifth team in the major leagues
to integrate. When the Braves left Boston after the 1952 season (they
moved to Milwaukee for the 1953 season), the Red Sox still had not signed
a black player. In fact, the Red Sox failed to integrate their team until
1959 when Elijah Jerry "Pumpsie" Green worked his way up through the
minor leagues to the Red Sox. The Red Sox were the last team in the
major leagues to integrate, which is not surprising considering the fact that
Green actually played for a manager who reportedly said, "There'll be no
niggers on this ball club if I have anything to do with it."[30]

The nation's racial relations in this period, and a sense of Boston's
inconsistent patterns of handling racial issues, professional athletics in
particular, brings us back to Willie O'Ree's integration of the National

Hockey League. The convergence of these contexts leads us to perhaps the most compelling reason for O'Ree's sparse attention in 1958—shame. Specifically, America was embarrassed that the "un-American" sport of hockey had integrated and, baseball, our "national pastime," still had a team clinging to segregationist practices. At a time when Boston and the entire country was in a tug-of-war with how it portrayed itself externally and the internal realities of the significance of race, bringing attention to hockey's progressive step would have only heightened the already intense pressure to remedy America's racial ills. Further, the fact that Boston was the host city for both the NHL's Bruins, the first team to integrate, and major league baseball's Red Sox, the last segregated team, was especially hard to accept. Who could provide a satisfactory explanation for this situation?

Because hockey was still primarily a regional sport in the United States, other sections of the country were less concerned about the issue than the few northeastern and midwestern locations with teams. Boston had nothing to gain and too much to lose by shining the light on O'Ree's achievement, as the Red Sox were already under tremendous scrutiny for fielding an all-white team. So rather than address the situation head on, society opted to push O'Rees's accomplishment aside and not deal with it until 40 years later.

The NHL should not be let off the hook either. Sure, the step was finally taken to allow a black player in the league, but facilitating and encouraging sustained access for players of color would be the true test. Until very recently, the NHL failed the test miserably. After O'Ree's brief exposure ended in 1961, there was not another black NHL player until Mike Marson played for the Washington Capitals in 1974. Further, league information shows that only 18 black players made it to the NHL from the time of O'Ree's first appearance in 1958 to 1991.

More recently, the NHL has made significant progress toward at least exposing more African Americans to the sport of hockey. In 2001, the NHL reported that 19 of its 650 players were black. Much of this noticeable improvement may be attributed to Canadian demographic shifts and the expansion of hockey in the United States. In the last 30 years, Canada's black population has risen from .02 to 2.0 percent. Although still a relatively small percentage, it is a significant increase. Also, the United States now supplies the NHL with approximately 15 percent of the league's players, but 30 years ago the contribution was minimal. But the best solution that the NHL has implemented to address this problem is the NHL/ USA Hockey Diversity initiative. Founded in 1995, this nonprofit program is designed to expose youth with limited resources to the sport of hockey. This important initiative has been introduced into 30 cities across the country and even includes an annual all-star game named after Willie O'Ree. The all-star game gives the 10- to 12-year-olds participating in the inner-city programs, mostly African American youth, the opportunity to be recognized for their citizenship, academics, and dedication to hockey. The NHL should be recognized for this step; however, the league should increase its involvement in the areas of financial assistance and development. In particular, the league should offer monetary support for the programs in each city (currently they do not). Otherwise, sustainability of such programs is unlikely, and developing a pipeline to higher level play will never occur (currently less than 1 percent of college hockey players are black).

TENNIS

The sport of tennis originated in France in the twelfth century. Although different countries derived their own names for the sport, Jeu de Paume (hand ball) in France, Royal or Lawn Tennis in England, and Royal Tennis in Australia, the one constant was the elitism associated with the game. Most early courts were, in fact, the courtyards of mansions or castles of the royalty who were the primary participants. Similarly, when tennis first arrived in the United States in 1874, it was available to an exclusively few, mainly the wealthy. The sport quickly became popular in the United States as it had in Europe, and by the early 1880s tennis club members had formed the United States National Lawn Tennis Association (USNLTA) as the sports governing body in America. The USNLTA maintained tennis's cloak of exclusivity, restricting membership in the same fashion that had become customary of country clubs and social groups in America. This, of course, meant that African American membership to the USNLTA was not an option. Nevertheless, like most every other sport introduced to this country, blacks found their own ways in which to participate.

By the end of the nineteenth century, blacks were already playing for more than recreation, organizing their own tennis clubs and holding their own competitive tournaments. The first of these tournaments was held in

1898 in Philadelphia. African American tennis clubs, primarily on the East Coast, continued to host invitation and interstate tournaments. Increasing interest and participation in tennis led African Americans to organize their own formal body on November 30, 1916. Known as the American Tennis Association, this association has the distinction of being the oldest African American sports organization in the United States, and continues to promote and support blacks' participation in tennis.[31]

The exclusivity of the United States Lawn Tennis Association (names had been shortened) did not dampen the spirits of the American Tennis Association (ATA). The ATA hosted its first National Championship Tournament in August 1917, in Baltimore, Maryland, at the Monumental Tennis Club. The three events held were Men's Singles, Women's Singles, and Men's Doubles. Tennis's segregation along racial lines was consistent with the status quo in American society throughout the 1920s and 1930s. On July 29, 1940, however, a major step was taken toward competitive, interracial tennis when Don Budge, considered the best player of the era, played Negro National Champion Jimmy McDaniel in New York City. Reportedly almost 2,000 onlookers saw Budge defeat McDaniel 6–1 and 6–2, but more important, the match was a starting point for the possibility of breaking the color barrier in tennis.[32]

It would take another full decade before the color line was officially broken. This occurred in 1950 when two-time winner of the black women's tennis championship Althea Gibson was granted the opportunity to play in the U.S. Nationals by the USLTA. Gibson lost in the second round of the tournament, but she defeated the racial mores of American society through her participation. And she went on to have a marvelous career in which she won 11 Grand Slam events and was inducted into the International Tennis Hall of Fame and the International Women's Sports Hall of Fame. Although Gibson always thought of herself as "just a tennis player" and not a spokesperson or representative for her race, her presence and successes on the tennis courts eliminated the USLTA's official policy of racial exclusion. As important, the fact that Gibson was a woman made her unique even among African American "firsts" in the sporting world.[33]

Despite Gibson's accomplishments as a tennis professional, it would be the late 1960s before another African American gained prominence in the tennis world. The player was Arthur Ashe. People began taking notice of Ashe's tennis talents in the late 1950s and early 1960s when he won boys' and men's ATA titles. But it was his National Collegiate Athletic Association title while a student at the University of California at Los Angeles in

1965 that gained Ashe national notoriety. Even this accomplishment was topped in 1968 when Ashe became the first American in 13 years to win the U.S. Open. Ashe went on to win many prestigious tennis tournaments and receive numerous honors throughout his professional career, including winning the All-England Wimbledon title in 1975 and serving as the non-playing captain of America's Davis Cup team from 1981–85.

Many assumed that Ashe's success as a tennis player was the final piece of the puzzle to eliminate tennis' reputation as an exclusive sport that was basically reserved for whites. The nation viewed itself differently than when Gibson arrived on the tennis scene; America had eliminated legal racial segregation through the *Brown v. Board of Education* case (1954), as well as the Civil Rights Act (1964) and Voting Rights Act (1965). Ashe was a man in a male-dominated society and sport. He had risen through the tennis ranks traditionally as a collegiate star at a prestigious university, and he even played the game with an elegance that tennis advocates enjoyed watching.

The combination of the social context and Ashe's personal attributes, however, has not been enough to bring about sufficient and sustainable change to tennis's racial profile since he entered center stage of the tennis world almost 40 years ago. Certainly the occasional black individual has emerged on the national tennis scene, but there have never been sufficient numbers to consider the individual more than simply an exception. Specifically, it would be interesting to survey those who consider themselves tennis advocates to name more than five African American players (male or female) who competed professionally in the last 25 years. There is little doubt that the percentage who could name more than five would be extremely low. The disappointing legacy of the lack of African American tennis players since pioneers like Gibson and Ashe is quite apparent, but less clear are explanations for why the sport remains virtually unchanged.

Like the aforementioned sports, tennis's answers and rationale are multifaceted. At the foundation remains the sport's tradition of economic and social privilege. Interest and potential success require early and sustained introduction to the game. This usually happens at the tennis/country club level, where not only are indoor and outdoor facilities available, but access to learning to play the game correctly is more likely. For most African Americans, acquiring the economic resources and social cache for such membership is unrealistic. This leaves most blacks who are interested in tennis with limited places to play. And for those who can find courts available to them year round, they cannot afford appropriate instruction.

2

HEROES OR VILLAINS? THE
CATEGORIZATION OF
AFRICAN AMERICAN STAR
ATHLETES, 1892–1946

In his compelling essay, "Be Like Mike? Michael Jordan and the Pedagogy of Desire," esteemed cultural critic Michael Dyson claims Jordan's rise to iconic status in much of African American culture rests on the shoulders of numerous black standout athletes who came before him. To capture the magnitude of these athletes' place in black life, Dyson states:

> Black sports heroes transcended the narrow boundaries of specific sports activities and garnered importance as icons of cultural excellence; symbolic figures who embodied social possibilities of success denied to other people of color. But they also captured and catalyzed the black cultural fetishization of sports as a means of expressing black cultural style, as a means of valoring craft as a marker of racial and self-expression, and as a means of pursuing social and economic mobility.[1]

Dyson's work on Michael Jordan is the next in a line of an important effort by scholars to explain how the role of outstanding African American athletes has always extended beyond the ring, court, or field. But after reading Dyson's explanation of the crucial place in black life that sport has traditionally held, one cannot help but wonder which great black athletes qualified for this "heroes" category?

When thinking about the great black athletes from the late nineteenth century through World War II who might be worthy of this status, most were considered controversial because of the circumstances of their sport, their own personalities, or both. In all cases, these premier athletes who were revered by some were in fact villainized by others. This difference in perception, however, does not necessarily invalidate Dyson's overall point of sports' comprehensive role in African American culture. Instead, if the term *villains* were substituted for *heroes*, and the phrase *cultural excellence* changed to *cultural chaos*, Dyson's assessment of star black athletes might still remain accurate. In other words, black athletes who escalated to the top of their respective sport, whether loved or hated, continued to be perceived as cultural icons who exemplified prominence and success (and the social and economic mobility that comes with it). Furthermore, when considering some of the most noted African American athletes of this era, and expanding the audience to black and white enthusiasts, we can better understand how the nation's preoccupation with sports intersected with race.

To explain why these athletes who displayed exemplary abilities in their given sport were revered by some and despised by others, it is imperative to address certain issues. First, and perhaps the most critical, is recognizing the relationship between historical context of the era in which the athletes reached stardom and assessing how consistent their perspectives and actions were with the racial mores of the time. Connected with the country's overall sentiment on racial issues are the cultural norms of the specific sport, the geographic region in which the athlete spent most of his time, and the athlete's conscious decision about what value he placed on public perception.

The three athletes who I will focus on are footballers William Henry Lewis and Paul Robeson and boxer Jack Johnson. Although there are a few others worthy of consideration, each of these black stars has been described as a premier athlete of his day and recognized for making unusual contributions to his chosen sport. Of interest, all three participated in either football or boxing. It should be noted that the decision to choose only football players and boxers was not merely a coincidence. Rather, these two sports, in part, reflect the limited athletic opportunities available to African Americans during this half-century era. But each also demonstrates the sports in which physical domination beyond the field or ring is reflective of society of the day. As scholar Gerald Early describes boxing, calling it "the most metaphorical drama of male neurosis ever imagined in the modern world," a similar argument fits the sport of football.

In 1900, the *AME Zion Quarterly Review* published an essay singing the praises of the path-breaking African American football player and coach, as well as prominent lawyer, William Henry Lewis. The *Review* said of Lewis: "Our race is proud of him because in all his success he stands for us, and the higher he goes in the physical field of athletics or the mental field of law or literature, he must necessarily open the way for others, and lift us all up at the same time."[2] Without question, blacks had reason to point to Lewis as a model for the possibilities of all members of the race. Although Lewis's accomplishments were in fact far removed from most African Americans at the turn of the century, many of his personal experiences were not atypical for blacks. Born to former slaves in Berkley, Virginia in 1868, Lewis spent his early years in the South during an era in which recently freed blacks had their recently distributed rights and privileges systematically withdrawn. The Reconstruction era witnessed the passing of the Thirteenth, Fourteenth, and Fifteenth Amendments between 1865 and 1870, giving blacks reason to believe that, at least legally, they would be recognized as free people, citizens, and have the rights and privileges associated with freedom. Yet this hope was short-lived, as the Compromise of 1877 represented the beginning of systematic (by law and by practice) efforts to limit economic opportunities, segregate socially, and restrict black suffrage.

Lewis's father, a Baptist preacher, managed to move the family to New England when Lewis was young in an attempt to escape the predetermined, subservient roles defined by southern society. Undoubtedly race-specific obstacles existed in the Northeast, but young Lewis managed to excel by hard work both in the classroom and on the football field. Lewis's commitment to education was evident by his willingness to work to pay for his education at Virginia Normal Institute (VNI), later named Virginia State University. From VNI he moved back North and attend prestigious Amherst College in Massachusetts. At Amherst, Lewis was one of the first African Americans to participate in college football and, in 1889, participated in the first recorded college football game in which a predominately white team fielded a team with black players.

Apparently he was considered more than just a good player by his teammates, as he was named team captain in 1890 and 1891. Moreover, Lewis was admired and respected by his classmates as indicated by his selection as orator at his graduation. Also, Lewis had gained the respect of educated black elite in the Northeast as indicated by the presence of

W.E.B. Du Bois and William Monroe Trotter to hear his speech. After graduating from Amherst College in 1892, Lewis attended Harvard Law School. It was not unusual to play football as a post-baccalaureate student during this era, so Lewis took advantage of the opportunity and continued to gain notoriety on the gridiron as well as in the halls of learning at Harvard. Lewis performed well enough to earn Walter Camp All-American status in 1892–93 and, after earning his law degree in 1895, served successfully as a coach of the Harvard football team while launching his legal and professional career in Boston.[3]

Being an All-American athlete who had recently earned a law degree from Harvard gave Lewis a rare distinction for African Americans at the end of the nineteenth century in Boston or any other city; that is, Lewis was given the benefit of the doubt. Certainly Lewis still had to prove himself in the competitive and complex worlds of law and politics, but because athletics allowed him to be viewed positively in the public sphere, he could focus more on the task at hand and, perhaps, worry less about whether or not people questioned his competency.

It was not long before Lewis parlayed his rise to recognition in college into a prominent place in the broader Boston community. First elected to the Cambridge City Council in 1899, Lewis went on to be elected to the Massachusetts state legislature in 1901. In 1903, he was appointed Assistant U.S. Attorney for Boston, and in 1907 while serving as head of the Naturalization Bureau for New England, Lewis was named Assistant U.S. Attorney for all of New England. The culmination of Lewis's political career came when he served as Assistant Attorney General of the United States from 1911 to 1913. Appointed to this position by President Taft, Lewis had the distinction of holding the highest federal appointment of any African American, a merit he could claim until the late 1930s.[4]

The abilities that Lewis displayed on the football field, first at Amherst and later at Harvard, make it easy to understand why sports fans admired him as an athlete. But there were numerous other excellent players who made Camp's All-American teams who never reached Lewis's acclaim for their contributions to the sport. The distinctions made between outstanding, African American football players and heroes like Lewis require a more in-depth analysis than just measuring dominance on the field. Certainly the aforementioned football credentials contributed to Lewis's elevation to greatness, but his ability to excel in the classroom was respected in the late nineteenth century just as it might be valued by many people today. This reflects how American society has always been fascinated with individuals who demonstrate exceptional skill in what are considered divergent areas. Thus Lewis's ability to dominate football games and earn degrees from two prestigious colleges at the same time automatically placed him in select company. Yet it was Lewis's display of another invaluable skill, one that arguably was even more important than his unusual athleticism and impressive intellect, which bolstered his reputation in numerous social circles; Lewis mastered the unique ability to navigate the delicate, interracial and intraracial interactions during an era when African Americans, even if they had the willingness and wherewithal, met opposition from whites and blacks.

Lewis's public notoriety, versatility with dealing with various types of people, and decision to engage them on their terms were important prerequisites for earning cross-racial respect. But even more was necessary to attain cross-racial heroic status. To reach this elite group, Lewis would need the support of someone who had already reached that category. Lewis received such an endorsement from the person recognized as the most influential African American leader of his time, Booker T. Washington. Without question, Washington's advocacy completed Lewis's "portfolio" and helped place him in the position to receive admiration and respect in his professional career just as he had as a scholar-athlete.

To appreciate the role of Washington's support, it is important to understand Washington's emergence to prominence as the ultimate "representative of the race." Born a mulatto slave in Virginia in 1856, Washington became the preeminent educational leader and political spokesman for African Americans by the turn of the twentieth century. His work ethic, vision, and astute cultural awareness of white persons of influence helped Washington found Tuskegee Institute in 1881. The school that he built quickly became known as the "Machine" for racial uplift, as well as the igniter of his own advancement politically.[5]

The topic where Washington was criticized most harshly, that of social progress for African Americans, was also the theme that propelled him into national prominence. Washington articulated his ideas on blacks' restricted social place in American society most clearly in his Atlanta Exposition Address in 1895. Described by Du Bois and others as the "Atlanta Compromise," Washington explained that blacks should worry less about their segregated and subsequently inferior position in society;

instead they should channel their limited resources toward the areas they could influence. Specifically, he contended that blacks needed to focus on making themselves a desirable labor pool for the South's emerging industrial economic culture. Du Bois and others responded with accusations of accommodationism, but Washington maintained his philosophy of what was best for the race and parlayed it into personal power and influence, especially among white elites.

Washington advocates argued that his willingness to defer racial advancement in the social and political arenas was a necessary compromise to help African Americans develop a solid economic foundation. Thus he managed to solicit previously unprecedented financial gifts from wealthy whites, which enabled Tuskegee and other historically black colleges and universities to make significant educational strides. Washington's dissenters, however, often considered his willingness to concede on fundamental rights such as the franchise and social equality as relinquishing principles of which no American citizen should have to surrender. Furthermore, although noted for assisting other schools with philanthropic ventures, Washington's critics contended that many of his decisions and actions were too heavily influenced by his preoccupation to remain the most prominent African American spokesman of the day rather than what was best for the black masses.

Regardless of the controversy surrounding Washington's philosophy for racial uplift, his acceptance by whites and his effectiveness in working with them had a tremendous impact on Lewis's rise to political recognition. In particular, it was Washington who gave President Roosevelt an endorsement of Lewis for Assistant District Attorney in Boston. And it was Washington's recommendation of Lewis to President Taft that prompted the Lewis ascendancy in the Taft administration.[6]

The importance of Washington's support of Lewis's political career is undeniable. At a time when few African American leaders were acknowledged by the white elite, Washington maintained access to the wealthy and political leaders of the day; he even raised the ire of the most liberal whites by having dinner at the White House with President Roosevelt in 1901. But Lewis's fortune of gaining Washington's support was no accident. Rather, it symbolized Lewis's conscious decision to continue practicing what had served him well in the past—work within a system acceptable to whites. In Lewis's case, the system was shaped and defined by Booker T. Washington.

Of interest, Washington and Lewis's relationship began on less than admirable terms, as Lewis had been critical of Washington's political strategies. Just a few years before Washington supported Lewis for a Presidential appointment, Lewis had discounted Washington among a group of educated Boston blacks, suggesting that Washington return back to the South and "leave to us the matters political affecting the race." Also in 1898, Lewis had allegedly called for people to "burn down Tuskegee," the school founded and led by Washington.[7] By 1901, Washington and Lewis had mended their fences and realized the mutual benefit of working together; Washington would have a respected African American advocate in Boston, an area where he faced much scrutiny, and Lewis's political career would flourish with Washington's approval.

Lewis's shift to devotee of Washington was most evident at a 1903 meeting chaired by Lewis to discuss the "status of the race." The meeting was sponsored by the National Negro Business League and was held at the Columbus Avenue A.M.E Zion church; Washington was the featured speaker. Like most of Washington's public speaking engagements, the meeting drew a wide variety of attendees, including Boston's most outspoken critic of Washington, William Monroe Trotter. The Harvard-educated Trotter founded an African American weekly newspaper, the *Guardian*, which he often used for his personal diatribes to promote black civil and political rights. Reportedly, Trotter jeered Washington relentlessly during his entire speech. As chairman, Lewis had the awkward task of acting as intermediary, literally and figuratively, between two authoritative voices in African American life in the early twentieth century. Lewis tried to maintain civility in the discussions, but according to Boston newspapers the next day, he lost control of the meeting and Trotter's alleged belligerent actions sparked a riot. The confrontation resulted in Trotter's arrest and, Lewis, the former outspoken critic of Washington himself, served as the chief witness for the prosecution.[8]

As expected, Lewis was perceived as an opportunist at best and race-traitor at worst by many African American anti-Washingtonians. In reference to Lewis, Trotter's newspaper, the *Guardian*, stated that, "His is a real case of being colored for leadership and revenue only."[9] Albeit harsh, it is easy to understand why critics might make such statements against Lewis. Leaders like Trotter understood that the likes of Lewis, those with notoriety and respect universally, were few and far between. Thus many leaders believed that if true progress in the struggle for equality was to occur, the race needed its designated spokesmen to articulate a similar message about what was best for blacks. From Trotter's perspective, this message should emphasize autonomy and self-sufficiency. But Washington's position was different; in the foreseeable future he would work within a system that deemphasized such characteristics. Given Lewis's history, especially since his days as an athlete at Amherst, it is not surprising that he would gain the favor of Washingtonians (black and white). Lewis had learned from his days at Amherst and Harvard that he was unique. Too few African Americans were afforded the opportunity to attend such prestigious schools, and even fewer enjoyed Lewis's athletic accomplishments once there. Thus Lewis had the privilege of working from a platform of success and accolades that came from football, and shaping it in virtually any way he wanted. To many, Lewis chose the path of least resistance by following Washington rather than someone like fellow Harvard alum, William Monroe Trotter. For Lewis's dissenters, his shift from condemning Washington previously to defending him in court was an easy target. Before dismissing Lewis as a traitor who chose individual success instead over racial progress, however, it is important to remember that Lewis had already been tapped as "special" by both races. This distinction brought with it such criticism for Washington and the handful of other late nineteenth- and early twentieth-century African Americans in this category.

Furthermore, although there is no proof that Lewis read the article written about him in the AME Zion Quarterly, he undoubtedly understood how athletics and education successes included certain obligations to the race; as the article suggests, "he must necessarily open the way for others." According to an early letter to Washington after they began working together, Lewis states, "If I could get a chance in Washington in the Department of Justice I feel I could 'make good' and put race prejudice to flight"[10] In Lewis's interpretation, paving a path for African American legitimacy meant using his foundation of athletic and intellectual respect among blacks and whites to achieve national presence in government, from which he might possibly make substantive change. Given the perpetual remnants of racial discrimination, it is difficult to access Lewis's success during his lifetime. But Lewis's accomplishments cannot be measured by narrow parameters. Evaluating Lewis's contributions must be grounded in the way that he used the football field as his platform to attain cross-racial support and respect during a time when African Americans rarely had the opportunity to do so. Lewis's mere presence at

Amherst and Harvard placed him in high regard among African Americans, and receiving Walter Camp All-American accolades on the gridiron put him in unprecedented company. But to reach and maintain true hero status, it was not sufficient just to impress his race. Lewis needed the endorsement of whites, which could occur only if they were comfortable with him in a broader context beyond sports and school. By aligning himself with Booker T. Washington and his racial philosophy, Lewis at least ensured that he had a chance to maximize the positives stemming from his athletic career.

Lewis's athletic accomplishments combined with his conscious decision to navigate the white rules of society were appreciated by many blacks and most all whites even more with the emergence of Jack Johnson on the sporting scene. Reigning as the heavyweight boxing champion of the world from 1908 to 1915, probably the country's quintessential representation of manhood and supremacy, Johnson experienced a very different reception than his fellow athletic standout, William Lewis. For sure, the two were perceived differently for legitimate reasons; Lewis was educated, articulate, and politically astute; Johnson spent few years in school, combined a southern drawl and slang when speaking, and displayed little regard for what people thought of his actions in or out of the ring. These characteristics have no direct correlation to either's dominance on the football field or in the boxing ring, but they had everything to do with their status as sports heroes or villains, as well as their influence on race relations.

Johnson's reputation, like Lewis's, was influenced by Booker T. Washington. By the time Johnson held boxing's most prestigious prize in 1908, Washington's position as the arbitrator of African American legitimacy was firmly in place. Washington's philosophy of gradual progress with minimal convergence with whites was at least acceptable to most blacks and applauded by whites. Yet Johnson's chosen path in life, especially during his seven years as heavyweight champion, modeled very few, if any, of Washington's established set of expectations. In fact, during Johnson's tenure in the boxing world's limelight, he became the epitome of Washington's greatest fear: representatives of the race whose actions brought pause to "Negro progress" in the eyes of society.

Despite rejecting the defined roles for blacks' social acceptance while heavyweight champion, Johnson's life began very much like the folks to whom Washington made his greatest appeal. Born in Galveston, Texas in

1878, Arthur John (Jack) Johnson, experienced the hand-to-mouth subsistence familiar to so many black southerners in the late nineteenth century. Likewise, at least one of his parents had been a slave and he came from a large family; his father, Henry, was a former slave, and his mother, Tiny, gave birth to six children. Also, Johnson displayed at a young age that he was not afraid of hard work. In fact, by the time Washington had established Tuskegee Institute and gotten the attention of white and black America, an observer might have concluded that Johnson had taken Washington's message of "pulling yourself up by your bootstraps" to heart. Although Johnson quit school by the sixth grade, he did so not to reinforce the stereotype of lazy and indolent behavior typically assigned to African Americans of the time. Instead, he had to sacrifice his childhood and go to work in the tough, arduous life of unskilled labor designated for the overwhelming majority of late nineteenth-century African Americans. This decision began a series of menial jobs worked by Johnson until he stumbled on the sport of boxing as a 16-year-old. Shortly after his exposure to the sport, Johnson began touring on the Negro boxing circuit, which translated into participating in vaudeville-like roles in addition to serious bouts to make a living. Johnson quickly committed himself to boxing and enjoyed a rapid ascendancy toward the Negro heavyweight title, earning that status in 1903.[11]

Johnson's significant achievement was bittersweet, as the title of Negro heavyweight champion of the world underscored the reality that he was prohibited from fighting for the "true" heavyweight title. The restrictions of Jim Crow in the early twentieth century meant that even if he were included in the annals of boxing history, his title would be viewed like everything else prefaced with the term Negro—second-class status. Johnson managed to eliminate this label in 1908 by navigating his way to a shot at the heavyweight championship of the world. He seized the moment of this unprecedented opportunity and defeated then champion Tommy Burns in a bout in Australia.

Johnson's monumental victory over Burns created euphoria for African Americans throughout the country. By winning boxing's heavyweight championship of the world, Johnson became a shining star during a particularly dismal era for blacks. The turn of the century brought with it a hope that racial equality would be a significant component of the country's reevaluation of itself. Instead blacks' desire for a fair place in society was met with continued intimidation and violence. Specifically, from 1900 to

1917, the period often referred to as the Progressive Era, approximately 1,500 African Americans, primarily men, were lynched. This ultimate act of control was reinforced by race riots in places such as Atlanta, Georgia; Brownsville, Texas; and Springfield, Illinois. Thus Johnson's tenure as boxing's best from 1908 to 1915 served as more than a proud moment in black sports history; it became a reservoir of temporary pleasure from the violence and racial tensions of day-to-day black life.

Johnson's presence in this most desirable place in sports and society in general was particularly important when considering black America's broader reactions to their plight in society. His winning of the title coincided with the birth of the National Association for the Advancement of Colored People (NAACP) and the National Urban League (NUL), the two organizations that would lead the rebuttal against antiblack sentiment. Founded in 1909, the NAACP became the foundation for challenging racial injustice through public and legal forums. One year later, the NUL was founded, and its mission to assist African Americans improve social conditions, primarily through economic independence, combined with the NAACP to help give black America the necessary foundation to meet the race's challenges of the time. The momentum of these two, prominent organizations was invaluable for the ongoing push for African American equality, but neither they nor any other advocacy group could prepare the country for the impact that Johnson would have on the interracial/intraracial conflicts during his stay at the top of the heavyweight boxing world.[12]

Johnson's exploits as boxing champion are well documented; his showmanship in the ring, blatant parading of white women in his personal life, and overall disregard for the race's rules of the day contributed to his infamous reputation. These controversial behaviors in his professional and personal life are typically referenced when considering his historical relevance. But in the context of why he was revered or hated, two interrelated issues are often overlooked or acknowledged only implicitly when analyzing Johnson's legacy; his "unforgivable blackness" and ingratitude of his exceptional status.[13]

Of interest, it was Johnson's focus on individual achievement and the personal accolades that came with winning the heavyweight championship that motivated him. In many ways, he had taken Washington's philosophy to heart by working hard and paying his dues before earning a measure of respect. But what Johnson failed to realize early on, and misunderstood or chose to disregard later, was that individual accomplishment transformed into collective identity without warning. Because of America's tradition of racial discrimination, any African American who excelled beyond the status quo had the weight of the race thrust upon his or her shoulders. For those African Americans like Johnson who had not been immersed in the conversations of racial uplift, this burden was perplexing, especially as even the most astute black leadership could not reach consensus on how the race could best capitalize on an individual's success.

In the words of race spokesman W.E.B. Du Bois, Johnson's boxing greatness and subsequent rise to public notoriety was almost predetermined to lead him to the category of "unforgivable blackness." Du Bois' premise is that once whites designated value to boxing, that is, an exemplar of superior athleticism and manhood, protecting it at all costs was intrinsic. Thus when Jack Johnson began his reign at the top of boxing, a rationale for why his athletic domination could not put him on par with his white boxer counterparts was necessary. The most convenient and easily acceptable explanation was to highlight Johnson's race. By doing so, the dominant American culture could deemphasize Johnson's apparent physical prowess by pointing to negative stereotypes assigned to African Americans from as far back as slavery. In particular, the focus became attacking Johnson's irresponsible behavior and lack of moral character.

Johnson's flash in the ring, often described as arrogant and disrespectful to his opponent, added insult to an already troubled white public. As well, many blacks were concerned about Johnson's antics, as they realized they were irritating to the white power structure. More problematic, however, was Johnson's disregard for the ultimate taboo: flaunting in public his relationships with white women. Best articulated by scholar Al-Tony Gilmore, Johnson's three marriages to white women and known sexual affairs with countless others created a national uproar. Such discontent culminated with charges of violating the Mann Act in 1912, transporting women across state lines for immoral purposes, when he traveled with a white woman, Belle Schreiber, whom he was involved with at the time. Although acquitted of the charges, Johnson's continuous disregard for the social mores of the time spurred the emotions of even the nonboxing fans.[14]

At the core of the fervor surrounding Johnson was his unashamed perpetuation of the stereotypes assigned to black men. Boisterous, ostentatious, and lustful of white women were descriptions that characterized Johnson during his championship years. Since the earliest days of slavery in America, these negative perceptions about black men were reinforced to justify racial inferiority. In essence, Johnson symbolized blackness. Such deep-rooted sentiment denied both blacks and whites the opportunity to access him on just his athletic accomplishments. People either hated or loved him for how he was, but more important, who he represented.

It was no surprise that whites villainized Johnson; to hear their jeers and read their negative commentaries against Johnson was to be expected. But as Gilmore highlights, the ferocious verbal attacks against Johnson, suggesting violent retaliation and questioning his worth as a human, symbolized a country obsessed with rejecting their greatest fears of black male superiority physically and sexually. One example that captures the intense reactions against Johnson comes from the Beaumont, Texas *Journal* newspaper writing, "The obnoxious stunts being featured by Jack Johnson are not only worthy of but demand, an overgrown dose of southern 'hospitality.'"[15] During the early 1900s, this type of hospitality, which usually meant violence or death, was the greatest fear for black folk. In the case of Jack Johnson, given his perceived appetite for white women and his literal and figurative towering over white men, the hospitality desired for him was to hang him from a tree with a noose around his neck.

Perhaps more fascinating is the conflicting opinions of hero and villain among African Americans. Johnson symbolized the debates of racial uplift ideology at its pinnacle. African Americans were struggling with questions about how to differentiate their individual and collective identities. Were their experiences black experiences, experiences by black people, or both? In many ways, Johnson forced blacks to answer these questions. Although they may have held a degree of pride about a black heavyweight champion, many blacks who voiced discontent for Johnson believed his character and moral flaws superseded his athletic accomplishments. And, during an era when it was common for any prominent black to carry the weight of the entire race on his/her shoulders, the legitimacy of the criticisms against Johnson was difficult to challenge for even his biggest boxing fans. Difficult because even though blacks despised the unfairness that came with the burden of representing the race, they understood the culture of the day. Best stated in a letter prepared by Booker T. Washington's personal secretary, Emmett Scott, for Washington, "No one can do so much injury to the Negro race as the Negro himself. This will seem to many persons unjust, but no one can doubt that it is true."[16]

To further complicate the dilemma that one individual, Jack Johnson, placed on African Americans in the early twentieth century, is that many blacks did indeed deplore his in the ring antics and out-of-the-ring life-style. Thus even if they appreciated the symbolic significance of having a black fighter hold the crown of heavyweight boxing champion, they were not obligated to support the individual holding the title. Yet even for those African Americans who viewed Johnson as a hero, the racial culture of the early twentieth century, primarily the relentless commitment to keep African Americans under the thumb of white superiority, reigned supreme in a way that even their cheers had to be tempered with a degree of humility.

Regardless of varying racial ideologies on what was the best course toward equality, a triad of circumstances in 1915 would prove devastating to even the most optimistic African Americans. In this single year, blacks would have to endure the death of Booker T. Washington, the race's most recognized and respected leader in black and white circles; the release of D. W. Griffith's *Birth of A Nation*, a film that reminded whites around the country why they needed to reclaim their country and, subsequently, pre-empted the revival of the Ku Klux Klan; and the end of Jack Johnson's seven-year run as heavyweight champion when he lost to "white hope" Jess Willard, confirming that whites were indeed superior. Such events made it imperative, perhaps more than any other time in the first two decades of the twentieth century, for the next generation of African American social consciousness and athletic prowess to emerge and reen-ergize the race. The person unsurpassed in either of these categories, and without question the exemplar of both, was Paul Robeson.

Born the youngest of seven children on April 9, 1898, in Princeton, New Jersey, Robeson grew up in a household that emphasized education, work ethic, and perseverance. Robeson's mother, Maria, died when he was a young child, leaving much of Paul's guidance in the hands of his father, Reverend William Robeson. A strict disciplinarian who was relentless in his demands, the elder Robeson urged his children to do their very best in everything they encountered in life. But rather than just preach these words, Rev. Robeson lived them himself. According to Paul, his father was a man with "rock-like strength and dignity," who never displayed a "hint of servility."[17]

Paul took his father's words and actions to heart, and maintained these fundamental principles throughout his life. Robeson's extraordinary talents as a student and athlete were evident during his schoolboy days in Westfield and Somerville, New Jersey. For example, as a student at Somerville High School, Robeson was a four-sport star, editor of the student newspaper, and member of the drama, glee, and debating clubs. At the same time, Paul maintained a solid A average in the classroom. He accomplished all of this as one of only three black students at a school of approximately 250 students.[18]

Probably because of the wisdom passed down by his father, Robeson realized that in his overwhelmingly white environment, people would measure and evaluate him on how he handled his exceptional status as a student-athlete rather than the accomplishments themselves. He understood the culture of white supremacy in early twentieth century America, which clearly differentiated between respect for what African Americans could do versus their recognition as equals in society. Robeson knew that by distinguishing himself from his white peers athletically *and* academically, he represented a disruption to the "natural order" of the racial hierarchy in America. This distinction was certainly unsettling to his white peers and those who knew him, so Robeson had to be careful not to alienate them when showcasing his superior talents. As Robeson later wrote in his autobiography, *Here I Stand*, "Above all, do nothing to give them cause to fear you, for then the oppressing hand, which might at times ease up a little, will surely become a fist to knock you down again!"[19] Through insights from his father and personal experiences along the way, Robeson was fully aware of the delicate balance between black pride and white acceptance he would need to navigate to reach hero acclaim in both complex and contradictory worlds.

Robeson would call on his father's lessons for survival and success often during his college years at Rutgers College. Despite the wishes of his family to attend Lincoln University, the oldest all-black college in the country and his father and brother's alma mater, Robeson opted for one of the state's elite white institutions. Clearly Robeson had incentive to attend Rutgers, as he had won a scholarship for his high score on a statewide examination. But Robeson's decision to attend Rutgers could not have been anticipated. Before his enrollment, only two blacks had ever attended Rutgers since it was founded in 1766, and when he arrived in the fall 1915 semester, he would be the only African American student on campus. Why, then, would Robeson opt to walk into a situation that had all the signs of racial exclusivity? As important, what made him think he might be successful?

Robeson already had dignity and self-respect, two values instilled in him by his father. But by the time of his entry into Rutgers, Robeson must have realized his unusual and multidimensional skills and talents, and he was bound to showcase them to a broad audience. In other words, Robeson understood that he had a different calling than most in life, one in which he was obligated to defy the cultural status quo that discouraged African American accomplishment in the white world. To do this, he would use his athletic and academic gifts to pave new trails for African Americans to follow and, at the same time, do so in a manner that kept whites comfortable with him.

"I don't want to have things handed to me. I don't want it made easy."[20] These words spoken by Robeson when deciding to attend Rutgers demonstrate an uncommon maturity for a 17-year-old. Yet unlike many at that age, Robeson had already experienced tremendous success as a student and athlete during an era when opportunities for African Americans were generally restricted to segregated schools and sports teams. Robeson's achievements were especially noteworthy when considering that he excelled in environments where few people, if any, looked like him.

On entering Rutgers, Robeson first confronted racism when he tried to join the football team. The school's legacy of admitting very few black students over the years was warning to Robeson of the trials and tribulations to come, and the intensity of such resentment would manifest most vividly on the football field. On reflection, perhaps this should not have been surprising given that Rutgers, like the overwhelming majority of white colleges and universities, had never fielded an African American on the gridiron. Robeson's attempt to break this color barrier was met with intimidation and down right nasty tactics to dissuade him from joining the team. As Robeson told the story, his first scrimmage with the team resulted in having his "nose broken, shoulder thrown out, and plenty of other cuts and bruises."[21] Robeson recalls his wounds taking 10 days to heal enough for him to return. In addition to his physical pain, Robeson was demoralized by such treatment, claiming that "I didn't know whether I could take any more."[22] Yet Robeson did return. He managed to gain strength to do so by recalling his father's lessons, concluding that "I was not there just on my own. I was the representative of a lot of Negro boys who wanted to play football, and wanted to go to college, and, as their representative, I had to show I could take whatever was handed out .... Our father wouldn't like to think that our family had a quitter in it."[23]

Robeson went on to gain the support and admiration of many of his football teammates; he was the first Rutgers footballer to earn All-American status in 1917–18, and earned an unprecedented 12 letters in four different sports during his college career. Robeson's athletic accolades brought him national notoriety, and black folk were especially proud to call "Robeson of Rutgers" one of their own. He was an inspiration to African Americans, perhaps more than any black athlete who preceded him, because of his role in debunking the myth of white superiority in sports. Robeson's physical talents could not be denied in part because he was so dominate on the football field, as well as a standout in basketball, baseball, and track, but mainly because he did so while competing at a white school against white athletes. Although Robeson's success on the football field (along with a few other blacks) did not lead to a preponderance of blacks playing at white universities immediately, it helped eradicate the standard practice of outright rejection solely because of race.

Yet Robeson's heroic status in the collegiate athletic world from 1915 to 1919 and his influence on the subsequent mores of college football were not due simply to his athleticism. Rather, his noted intellectual acumen and social sophistication transitioned him from famous to infamous status. In the scholastic arena at Rutgers, Robeson joined numerous social and academic clubs, as well as excelling in the classroom. His scholarly recognition reached its pinnacle during his senior year when he was selected as valedictorian, named one of only four men inducted into the college's exclusive Cap and Skull honor society, and asked to give the commencement address at graduation. The school newspaper, *Targum*, captured the sentiment of Robeson's peers at Rutgers, predicting that "He has dimmed the fame of Booker T. Washington and is the leader of the colored race in America."[24]

Such acclaim in 1919 was particularly unusual for a black man given the interracial friction at the close of World War I. Dubbed the "Red Summer" by writer James Weldon Johnson, from June 1919 to the end of the year the country witnessed approximately 25 race riots. This unprecedented racial unrest was a combination of increased expectations by African Americans after their service in the war and white reluctance to recognize them as equal citizens.

Despite the uncertainty of race relations, and similar to William Henry Lewis's experiences at Amherst, Robeson was aware of the national tenor during his collegiate years. He understood who he represented and the implications of his success or failure at Rutgers. Thus he practiced an uncommon public humility as to not draw the eye of envy from his peers at Rutgers. He regularly downplayed situations of racial discrimination or signs of inequity while at Rutgers. In one situation in which a local establishment would not serve him because of his race, Robeson claimed that he "wanted no trouble" rather than let his white peers protest the policy.

Robeson's athletic and academic accolades at Rutgers earned him national acclaim from all circles. To African Americans in particular, Robeson not only carried the burden of "pioneer" at Rutgers with courage and resiliency, he seemed to thrive on the challenges that came with representing the race. His unparalleled successes represented the model for the quintessential "Renaissance man" for the first two decades of the twentieth century. And to whites, as was reflected in the respect and admiration of his classmates at Rutgers, Robeson epitomized the type of person all blacks should aspire to model.

Robeson would play professional football for a few years after leaving Rutgers. Although professional football had not received the notoriety as did the college game, Robeson was an important name for the newly-established National Football League, as well as one of the league's first black players. Robeson also attended law school at Columbia University while playing professionally, earning his degree in 1923. Rather than launch a legal career, the versatile Robeson followed his true passions and channeled his energy toward the acting and singing professions, where he soon earned national and worldwide acclaim for his other talents. By all indications Robeson made a graceful transition from a remarkable athletic career to maintain his rare status of admiration in the African American and white worlds; he broke color barriers in film and theatrical roles; performed concerts in worldwide venues; and, was a public spokesman for pride, dignity, and civil rights for all forced into subservient status. Yet it would be his emphasis on the latter that would lead to the dramatic shift from hero to villain in the eyes of many in the nation.

As the 1920s unfolded, Robeson and other African Americans had reason to believe and expect that they would be treated differently in the United States now that approximately 1 million blacks had fought for freedom abroad. They were anxious to experience equal access to jobs, housing, and voting rights—all necessary ingredients for a true democracy—in their own country. Unfortunately the conditions for African Americans had little meaningful and substantive change after the war, leaving most disappointed and feeling betrayed by the country. Such dissatisfaction resulted in unprecedented protests by black leaders as well as common folk who demanded what they deserved—a fair shake in society.

One avenue in which black social, political, and economic concerns were addressed was through an explosion in the African American arts and music community. Thus the Harlem Renaissance (or rebirth) was born as an outlet and expression of African American humanity. And, just as he had done through his accomplishments at Rutgers as a scholar-athlete, Robeson would gain notoriety as a brilliant actor and singer and be a pioneer in this era of creativity with a cause. For example, in 1924, he played the leading role in *All God's Chillun Got Wings*, making him the first black man with a principal role beside a white woman in American history.[25]

Robeson would continue to be a darling on the national and international theatrical and musical scene throughout the 1920s and 1930s. In the context of race relations, his reputation as the consummate professional would land him the role of Othello on Broadway in 1943. African Americans could take pride in his tremendous success, all the while maintaining his quest for racial justice. Ranging from supporting the effort of labor unions, to meeting with major league baseball commissioner Kennesaw Mountain Landis about the desegregation of baseball, Robeson had evidence that he was compelled to use his public persona as a platform for worldwide civil rights. That Robeson was showered with support reinforced that he was still a national hero. Examples of his national appeal from 1943 to 1945 included being labeled "America's No. 1 Negro" by *American Magazine*, hailed as "the tallest tree in our forest" by African American spokeswoman Mary McLeod Bethune, and receiving the Spingarn Medal, the NAACP's highest honor to an individual.

But as Martin Duberman points out, "The Spingarn Medal marked both the apex of Robeson's public acclaim and the onset of his fall from official grace."[26] As the country adjusted to the new world order after World War II, Robeson's efforts to condemn what he described as fascism (at home and abroad) was admired by some, but drew the ire of many who deemed his outspokenness as "un-American." After voicing his discontent for the "colonial peoples" around the world in 1949 at the Congress of the World Partisans of Peace in Paris, Robeson suffered a devastating blow to his image. Almost immediately, Robeson went from one of few beloved African American figures across racial lines to a

shunned figure few would support publicly. Whites vilified him as a traitor to his country, and even Ms. Bethune, who praised Robeson a few
years earlier, stated that Robeson "does not speak for the National Council, and I am not aware that any other national Negro organization has
appointed or designated him to speak for them in Paris."[27] In addition to
waning support for Robeson's opinions, his opportunities for earning a
living as an actor and singer, at home or abroad, were disappearing rap-
idly. By the summer of 1950, he had lost his passport, precluding him
from international travel, as well as enduring the cancellation of numerous
scheduled domestic engagements.

Much of the public scrutiny aimed at Robeson was portrayed as his
ungratefulness to a country that had given him royalty-like treatment
over the years. But Americans should not have been totally surprised by
his adamant objections of the social order. For sure Robeson had become
more assertive in voicing his displeasure with worldwide inequity, but he
had never hid his desire for equality. In his commencement address in
1919 as the revered student-athlete at Rutgers, Robeson told the school's
president that to "touch upon the race question" was "burning in his soul
for expression."[28] And in his words, Robeson confirmed that his generation must struggle for peace, fight against poverty, prejudice, and the
demoralization of the human spirit. The disconnection was how he deliv-
ered his message and how people chose to interpret his words. In 1919,
Robeson was still a young man finding his way in society; thus he was
confined by the mores of the day. That is, he had to remain mindful not
to alienate whites and more conservative blacks when speaking out. Yet
Robeson was not vague in articulating that his life's work would be aimed
toward uplifting the downtrodden peoples of the world. Instead African
Americans and whites alike were captivated by his comprehensive bril-
liance, and focused on what he represented rather than stood for. To
whites, he modeled the humility they desired from all blacks—and if
someone of Robeson's standing remembered his place then certainly all
other blacks should model his behavior. For African Americans, Robeson
proved that they could be as good as, if not better, than whites in two
arenas where blacks were assumed inferior.

But as Robeson got older and the context of the social issues of the day
evolved, the integrity and determination that people admired in him previously became the points of his social disapproval. Perhaps the best way
to describe Robeson's demise is the dismissal of his contributions from

public memory by Rutgers, college football, and society at large. When the Rutgers *Athletic News* published the school's 65 greatest football players of all-time in 1954, Robeson was not included on the list. Also, Robeson's name was noticeably absent for consideration into the College Football Hall of Fame until a group finally nominated him in 1970. Despite submitting his name every year, he would not be inducted until 1995, 75 years after his collegiate career ended.[29]

Robeson's initial prominence came at a time when whites and many blacks were searching for an elite African American athlete to displace Jack Johnson. In Robeson they found the perfect heir apparent. Not only was Robeson a four-sport star who dominated the college football game, but he possessed an intelligence and dignity second to none. Yet it was this total package that the country showered with praise early on that would ultimately push beyond the limits of the status quo. I am sure that Robeson's graduating class at Rutgers figured they were paying him the utmost compliment when they predicted that he would one day become the governor of New Jersey. Although he was probably somewhat flattered by such a forecast, little did they know that he was motivated more by living in a society where all the citizens of New Jersey could vote for him or any other candidate in this hypothetical election.

The experiences of these three, gifted African American athletes highlight the complex intersection of the influence of race and the role of sports from the late nineteenth century through World War II. Each carried the burden of race, consciously or otherwise, in their athletic and personal decisions, and was forced to do so at the exposure of American society. In the cases of Lewis and Robeson, they seemed to realize that the pedestal of athletic heroism was to be used for greater good for the race. Contrarily, Johnson focused on what he wanted out of life, tremendous criticism notwithstanding, and worried much less about how his individual actions affected the race.

Because of Johnson's renegade lifestyle and seemingly carefree attitude about society's rules, it is easy to think of him as the prototypical "bad nigger." The controversies surrounding Johnson inside and outside the boxing ring enabled most whites and many African Americans to discount his athletic accomplishments. To remain in the envied position of heavyweight champion for seven years to the disgruntlement of much of the country was no small feat. But because he was a maverick, and because he reigned supreme in the sport that was the supposed to be the greatest example of athletic inferiority for blacks, reflections on Johnson's legacy will never be an objective exercise. And because Johnson followed Lewis, one of the early models for what the country envisioned for its black athletes, and was a contemporary of "Robeson of Rutgers," America's fascination with him will always be in the context of malevolence for his manner first and his athletic feats second.

To a certain degree, perhaps the same analyses hold true even when considering Lewis and Robeson. The major difference was that more was expected of Lewis and Robeson. Their backgrounds and the experiences that shaped them were strikingly similar to each other but in contrast to those of Johnson who was poor, uneducated, and southern. These qualities lessoned society's expectations, but it made him more familiar to the typical African American in the early twentieth century. As a result, he enjoyed a kinship with the black masses that allowed for much unconditional support throughout his career. On the other hand, Lewis and Robeson had been sanctioned as the ideal African American athletes who maintained class, intelligence, and professionalism at all times. Despite their prominence, they were oddities in comparison to the average African American of the day, perhaps making it more difficult for most blacks to relate to their predicaments. Of interest, Lewis and Robeson were the sons of preachers who left the South seeking better conditions for their children. Also, both were taught the importance of dignity and education, named Walter Camp All-Americans at predominately white schools, spokesmen at their college graduations, and recipients of prestigious law degrees.

Although Lewis and Robeson felt a sense of responsibility to represent the race positively, ultimately both found out that it was impossible to be all things to all people, especially if most of the people represented had such dramatically different life experiences. Still, both experienced harsh criticisms from the black elite as well. Lewis was often labeled too passive and Robeson deemed too aggressive. Lewis was considered an opportunist who conceded to the white power structure for personal benefit; Robeson was condemned for challenging American racism through the lens of international social, economic, and political practices. In Robeson's case, he forfeited his respected status with whites as well. Yet both had the conviction to use their hero status as athletes as a platform for racial advancement beyond individual examples. For this they should be remembered as heroic citizens first and premier athletes second when analyzing African American athletes in the first half of the twentieth century.

3

❦

WHEN THE ROOSTER CROWS: AFRICAN AMERICAN ATHLETES IN THE STRUGGLE FOR CIVIL RIGHTS, 1954–1968

In a 1964 press conference in Miami, Florida, just two days after defeating Sonny Liston for the heavyweight championship of the world, Cassius Clay responded to a barrage of questions about his affiliation with the Nation of Islam. Questioned about the religion's legitimacy and quizzed about his decision to practice the faith, Clay claimed that, "A rooster crows only when it sees the light. Put him in the dark and he'll never crow. I have seen the light and I'm crowing."[1] Clay's remarks captured a spirit that not only reflected his personal religious journey, but also embodied a sentiment among African Americans that had been growing toward collective action for at least a decade. In other words, African Americans throughout the country had begun to challenge racial injustice with an unprecedented intensity and determination. The interplay between sports stardom and sociopolitical involvement was a burden for almost every black athlete in the national limelight before Clay, but his encounter occurred during this era of resistance known as the Civil Rights movement.

Undoubtedly the most racially confrontational time in American history, this period augmented the fight against racial injustice coming out of World War II. As demonstrated by Paul Robeson's willingness to jeopardize his individual standing, and the concentrated efforts by society to push him from his perch, the rules of the day reflected that whether or not you are the premier African American scholar-athlete, blacks' attempts to reach beyond the status quo were still unacceptable. Yet until his death in 1976, Robeson's lifelong relentless spirit and reluctance to defer to inequity inspired the generation of athletes who emerged in the second half of the twentieth century.

When examining the Civil Rights movement, three questions always surface that influence what one concludes about the era: When did the movement begin? Was it successful? Who made the most significant contributions? Although these remain the magic questions that we still ponder today, most scholars agree that there are really no definitive answers. Black activists' intentions to become more shrewd and assertive were most successful during and after World War II, but they had been in process since the first decade of the twentieth century. As Roy Wilkins, past executive director of the NAACP stated, "The Negro of 1956 who stands on his own two feet is not a new Negro; he is the grandson or the great grandson of the men who hated slavery. By his own hands, through his own struggles, in his own organized groups—of churches, fraternal societies, the NAACP and others—he has fought his way to the place he now stands."[2]

Nonetheless, the one event that virtually everyone accepts as a benchmark in understanding Civil Rights history is the *Brown v. Board of Education* United States Supreme Court decision. Hailed by many as the most important court case of the twentieth century, the announcement that "separate but equal" was unconstitutional changed forever how American society would think, at least legally, about interactions between blacks and whites. Although countless efforts had been made previously and numerous strategies were in progress, this decision provided the foundation that gave Civil Rights leadership and organizations the momentum to press onward in their attempts to radically change the status of blacks in America.

The first prominent activist situation to attain national attention after the Brown decision was the Montgomery, Alabama bus boycott. Started in December 1955, and led by the Montgomery Improvement Association and its new president, Martin Luther King, Jr., a quiet but committed woman named Rosa Parks, and a host of other black Montgomerians, blacks demonstrated a readiness to fight the institutionalized racism of the South. Their collective efforts to thwart racial inequality in the "cradle of the Confederacy," inspired African Americans throughout the country, and seized the consciousness of three black pioneers in American sports,

Bill Russell, Jim Brown, and Cassius Clay. In turn, the courageous and challenging actions of these three athletic standouts inspired other black athletes and African American citizens to remain strong in their quest for equality.

When thinking about racial unrest and the influence of sports, people typically point to 1968 as the beginning of the politicized black athlete. Sports scholar David Wiggins's aptly titled chapter, "The Year of Awakening" in his book *Glory Bound*, clearly demonstrates that 1968 was a turbulent year for the United States. Dr. Martin Luther King, Jr. was assassinated, international protests against apartheid were staged through the threat to boycott the Olympics, and the public dismissal of the United States' anthem and flag by sprinters Tommie Smith and John Carlos remain vivid in the minds of many Americans. When considering these athletic and nonathletic events among numerous others, Wiggins is certainly right to anoint 1968 as a memorable year in understanding the connections among race, sports, and American culture. Yet similar to African Americans' battles for equal rights outside of sports, 1968 was more of a culmination of many years of struggling at what now seems like a snail's pace to earn any recognition rather than the time that they "woke up" in the world of athletics.[3]

African American athletes became more strategic and outspoken by the 1950s. Specifically, from 1956 to 1960, Bill Russell, Jim Brown, and Cassius Clay emerged on the professional sports scene as the catalysts for this "great awakening" of the new generation of black sports stars by the late 1960s. Outside of these three, few had the combination of national charisma and athletic accomplishments to command an audience for their every move. Their outspoken and principled demeanor on issues related to civil rights helped change the faces of their individual sports of basketball, football, and boxing as well as overall athletics. Exploring the trials and tribulations of these three unforgettable athletes, who had a tremendous amount to lose by challenging the status quo, highlight the national discontent in America for these two decades. Further, the situations these three men faced and the actions they took set important guides for how African American athletes would respond in the next 30 years. Perhaps more important, their actions also influenced how society might respond to the powerful personalities of the black athletes to come.

In 1974, William Felton Russell was selected to the Basketball Hall of Fame. In the basketball world, such recognition is a tremendous honor and deemed the sports' highest complement. When the selection committee announced its 1974 inductee class, it was especially proud because the group included this great Boston Celtics player. Choosing Russell from an accomplishment or performance standpoint was not the reason the Hall gleamed; rather, in choosing Russell, the Hall had extended its hand for the first time to a black basketball player. To the Hall of Fame this symbolized progress for race relations in the sports world. The Hall assumed that Russell would be as gratified about the news as they were, but as had been the case in so many instances, they miscalculated what was important to Russell. Russell viewed the alleged honor differently. His immediate reaction was to issue a simple statement saying that for "personal reasons" he preferred not to be inducted.

In his autobiography, *Second Wind: The Memoirs of an Opinionated Man*, Russell reveals that one of the deterrents against joining the Hall of Fame was affiliation with some of its members. In particular, he refused to have his legacy associated with legendary basketball coach Adolph Rupp. Rupp, who built a basketball dynasty at the University of Kentucky, was known as a staunch racist and proponent of segregated intercollegiate athletics. In speaking about Rupp, Russell claimed, "I acknowledge that Adolph Rupp did a lot for basketball, and perhaps he deserves to be in the Hall of Fame. But I did not want to be associated with him or anybody else of his racial views. I saw that as my free choice to make."[4] Russell's decision to snub the Hall of Fame and his outspoken criticism of Rupp captured his willingness to stand up for his beliefs, regardless of what others thought about him.

As a result of the decision to shun his induction into the Hall of Fame, Russell was widely and harshly criticized for his presumed indifference about an honor that much of America had deemed sacred. Yet in reconsidering this decision and several others during Russell's 13 seasons with the Celtics (1956 to 1969), a one-word description with two interrelated traits emerges about him—pride. Russell always exuded tremendous pride in himself as a human, American, and person of African descent, and his collective sense of identity often manifested itself through his conviction and courage. Russell thought carefully about the forthcoming public onslaught he would receive for his reaction to the Hall; he even expressed that he occasionally second-guessed his decision, saying to himself: "Hey, lighten up. You're making too big a deal out of this. Just put the best face on it, and let it go."[5] But in such moments Russell also reminded himself how strongly he felt and how carefully he had thought about the matter; he trusted his decision and was not swayed.

Russell rejected the label of role model attached to him during his basketball-playing days, but during his tenure with the Celtics, it was virtually impossible for black society to view him any other way. The legacy of racism that prevailed in American culture prevented all but a few black athletes to have a voice in the mid-1950s when Russell arrived on the professional basketball scene, and an even smaller number had the opportunity to express their sentiments about civil rights before World War II. But Russell's words were thoughtful and poignant, and his actions were often atypical.

Many people, especially the white sportswriters and Celtics fans in the Northeast could never seem to figure out their great basketball star. They cheered his leadership and tenacity on the court, but off the court they shook their head in dismay when he unleashed one of his piercing commentaries on race issues or displayed his cool and distant demeanor in public. People could not understand why this praised sports star never embraced what they viewed as the warmest of receptions. Instead, early on in his career he said, "You owe the public the same thing it owes you. Nothing."[6] Ultimately his manner left most people somewhere between uncomfortable with, or resentful of, Bill Russell the person. Certainly Russell could be enigmatic at times during his playing days with the Celtics. Even his teammates struggled with handling his jovial and playful ways on some days followed by withdrawing from them on others. But when taking a closer look at Russell's life experiences before joining the Celtics, and the context of the era when he starred for the team, it becomes easier to understand Russell's complexity.

Bill Russell was born February 12, 1934, in Monroe, Louisiana, to Charlie and Katie Russell. For blacks born and living in the Jim Crow South during the era just after the Great Depression, it was impossible not to witness and experience blatant racism and injustice. Negative reactions to black male–white female relationships, sexual exploitation against black women, restricted job options, and adult blacks deferring to white youth were everyday occurrences. The Russell family was no exception to these rules. But respect was one important element that the Russell family maintained in the Monroe black community. Admiration for the Russell family began with Charlie's father and Bill's grandfather. Mr. Russell, who Bill affectionately referred to as "the Old Man," could not read or write, but he was able to earn a living without ever working for anyone. It was a rare occasion for a black man living in the South to support his family without answering to whites.

Russell's father, Charlie, worked in a "negro job" in a local paper factory, and the family had very few extras. In the first sentence of *Second Wind*, Russell describes his father as a strong man. Charlie, standing 6 foot 2 inches and weighing more than 200 pounds, was definitely a physical presence. But his true strength rested in how he related to his family and the local black community. Russell recalls, "To his kinfolk scattered across northern Louisiana, Mister Charlie was someone to count on for strength, wisdom and good humor."[7] A part of the high regard for Charlie was because of his audacity to "eye-ball" white folks who disrespected him or his family. One example occurred at a gas station when Russell was a young boy. The white attendant at the station intentionally made Charlie wait to pay for his gas while he carried on conversations and pumped gas for other white customers. Finally, when Charlie had seen enough, he threatened to drive off from the station without paying the attendant. The attendant saw Charlie and rushed up to him, screaming epithets and calling him "boy" in front of his family. Charlie responded by grabbing a tire iron and chasing the attendant down the street. Thankfully he did not catch him. For years Charlie would speak regretfully about the situation, not because he stood up to protect his human dignity in front of his family, but because in challenging the southern custom of black subservience he potentially threatened the welfare of himself and his family. Frustrated by such experiences, soon thereafter Charlie and his family left the South for good.

Russell's mother, Katie, died unexpectedly at the young age of 32. He was only 12 years old at the time, but she had already left a lasting impression about the importance of pride and dignity. In reflecting on memories of his mother, Russell remembers how, when he was 9 years old, she made him literally fight for respect in his new West Oakland, California, neighborhood. Russell recalls how insignificant it was to win these childhood battles in comparison to his mother's support, claiming that "the scrapes and bruises were nothing compared to my mother's proud approval."[8]

The stubbornness, work ethic, and assertiveness modeled for Russell by the three most influential people in his childhood remained with Bill Russell the adult. He had watched his parents and grandfather experience racial injustice and do the best they could to rebuff it during an era when

African Americans took tremendous risks for trying. So when Russell reached the athlete's pinnacle by becoming a professional, and even a superstar, it now seems difficult to imagine that he would not hold onto the characteristics instilled in him by his grandfather, father, and mother and speak out against racism when he witnessed it.

Speak out, both verbally and in his actions, is exactly what Russell did during the period from 1963 to 1965. By his own admission, Russell had become somewhat bored with basketball. And like so many other promi-nent African Americans, he put aside some of his individual situations and began focusing on the greater cause of decent treatment and equal access for all blacks in America. As he eloquently stated, "How could I 'play' basketball as a grown man in the same way I had played it as a kid, when there were so many more important things going on?"[9] As a man of principle, he was exactly right. How could he sit idly on the sidelines after the student sit-ins in Greensboro, North Carolina, the marches in Birmingham, Alabama, and the voting rights initiatives in Mississippi?

Russell claimed that his reactions to prejudice had always been a mix-ture of laughter and rage. When people offended him, Russell's response to offensive statements or actions, depending on whether he was having a good or bad day, ranged from laughing, scowling, or lecturing. The words and actions of leaders such as Malcolm X and Dr. King seemed to inspire Russell to become even more outwardly critical of the United States and Boston in particular. In other words, he began to display more regularly attitudes closer to rage than laughter. Russell's brazenness led to actions such as challenging a Boston newspaper to quote him calling Boston "the most racist city in the United States."[10] He also availed his support of the Civil Rights cause nationally by appearing in Mississippi after the murders of Civil Rights workers James Chaney, Andrew Goodman, and Michael Schwerner during the summer of 1964.

Indeed, by this time Russell was a role model and, dare I say, hero, to many African Americans. Just two years after returning to the South, the place that had changed very little in the 30 years since he was born there, Russell accomplished perhaps his greatest accomplishment for racial jus-tice. He was named player-coach of the Boston Celtics. Although "player" appeared first in his title, to African Americans "coach" was the only description that mattered. Russell had become the first black head coach of any major American professional sport. More important, he had done it his own way, despite the criticism and second-guessing that came with his unpopular opinions and, at times, unpleasant demeanor. Russell represented to African Americans that someone like many of them could rise to the top on his or her terms, albeit rarely. His statements in the early 1960s addressing race relations in America capture what he saw as the underpinning problem. Russell contended that "The basic problem in Negro America is the destruction of race pride. One could say we have been victims of psychological warfare, in a sense, in that this is a white country, and all emphasis is on being white."[11] Through his efforts as a player and coach, and his willingness to speak out against injustice, Russell did more than his part to reinstill racial pride back into America.

In his 1964 autobiography, *Off My Chest*, football great Jim Brown captured the sentiments of Russell and, perhaps, other black athletes and African Americans throughout the country, claiming "My views—strong views—are not original, yet I am in a better position than most Negroes to attempt to awaken the white man to the fact that the time is not tomorrow but now. I'm one of those niggers who 'ought to be glad to be here.' I make big money. I enjoy fame and even adulation. My future is assured. Nevertheless, I am not thankful to be here. If anything, I am more angry than the Negro who can't find work."[12] Brown's words reflect the frustration that he had encountered as a recognizable black athlete since he began his college career in 1953 and, as the title of his book suggests, he saw this as an opportunity to get some of his personal experiences and thoughts on society's overall racial situation out in the open. To assess Brown's journey to becoming arguably the best running back in professional football history, as well as the most outspoken African American football player during his playing days, it is important to understand his interpretation of how the conditions for blacks in football and in America influenced each other.

Brown was born in 1936 on St. Simons Island off the southern coast of Georgia. Describing his birthplace as "an undiscovered thing of beauty," Brown has mostly pleasant memories of his early childhood in this deep South community. Such recollections were no guarantee given that Brown's guardian for most of his early years was his great-grandmother. Brown's father deserted the family shortly after his birth and his mother left seeking better opportunities in New York when he was only two years old. But Brown lived in a four-bedroom house shared by several relatives, and received the love and discipline that allowed for a relatively happy childhood. He recalls interacting regularly with white children and thought little of the fact that he attended a segregated school.[13]

Brown's familiarity with whites probably eased the transition of moving to the North to live with his mother at age nine. Brown spent most of the next several years in the Manhasset community on Long Island and was educated at majority white Manhasset High School. He enjoyed a tremendous athletic career at Manhasset, playing five sports and earning 13 letters, and seemed to fit in fairly well with his peers. Brown's athletic accomplishment led to numerous scholarship offers from universities across the country; by his count he had 45 offers.

To the surprise of many, Brown decided to continue his education and athletic career at Syracuse University. Many expected that he would attend one of college football's powers such as Ohio State or Michigan. His decision proved to be eye-opening, particularly as it related to his status as a black man. From the beginning it was apparent to Brown that he would be viewed differently at Syracuse than he was at Manhasset. He struggled with the adjustments of big-time college football, but the more surprising challenge was dealing with the discrimination at the school. Brown had managed to get along fine with whites in high school, so he expected no racial problems at Syracuse even though he was the only African American player on the football team when he arrived in 1953. But he was wrong, and the complexity of race-related experiences in college seemed to awaken Brown to issues that did not make sense to him. As he describes it, "I met all those loving white people at Manhasset. Then I went to Syracuse, ran chin first into overt racism. Someone had changed all the rules, and (sic) forgotten to tell me."[14]

What seemed most surprising and troubling to Brown was that he was no longer judged as an individual on his own merits. Now it was as if he bore the responsibility of an entire race on his shoulders. In *Off My Chest*, Brown discusses the reputation of a former black football player at Syracuse, fictitiously named Marion Francis. Francis allegedly had too much mouth and was too friendly with the white coeds for a black man while at Syracuse. The problem for Brown was that he was bombarded with "Don't be like Marion Francis" comments from his earliest days on campus. In his thinking, why was he the only guy who received such warnings? Was it because Francis was black, too? Such questions irked Brown, as he had "come to Syracuse to get an education and play sports. I had not come to date white girls."[15] Brown would continue to be reminded of the sins of

Francis. He would never become comfortable with the comparisons, not because Francis was a bad person, but because Brown resented being judged on some criterion other than his own. Brown stated it best, claiming that "I always felt like an animal who was being tolerated in the living room as long as he didn't shed hair on the sofa."[16]

For the most part Brown shrugged off the comparisons to Francis or anyone else who he believed was referenced to him just because they were African American. But he never forgot the negative feeling when it happened or accepted racial generalizations of him as an individual when others tried to categorize him. Even more, the exposure to blatant racism at Syracuse, or at least a degree that he was not anticipating, would continue to influence his reactions to racial bigotry. While still a student at Syracuse, Brown had returned to St. Simon Island to visit family when he was reminded that even in the place where he was comfortable as a child, he was a black man with the restrictions that come with it first and superstar athlete second. He recalls honoring the request to meet the man of the house where his grandmother worked. Brown remembers exchanging pleasantries and the gentleman stating how proud the folks of St. Simons Island were of him. What bothered Brown was the reluctance of the gentleman to invite him into his house, stating that "he's glad to meet me, but I'm not worthy of common courtesy."[17] Brown contends that he was more sad than angry about being acknowledged as a football star but disrespected as a black man.

For years Brown refused to return to St. Simons Island after this experience. The place where he had fond memories as a child had let him down just like his experience at Syracuse. He had been duped in both contexts; he was an object—an animal-like football player—rather than a person. Brown rejected society's incongruous perceptions and treatment aimed at him and other African Americans, and made his sentiments public after he joined professional football in 1957. He voiced his refusal to be the warrior on the field and turn into the passive Negro that America was comfortable with after the game was over, asking the question, "How could I have the courage to run that hard, then be so weak off the field that I'd succumb to inequity."[18]

Perhaps Brown's most important attribute for his activism and assertiveness during his tenure as a professional football star was that he understood the significance of history of blacks' experiences in America. Brown knew that African Americans had a legacy of assumed inferiority, and that even when someone like him excelled, he was merely thought of as an exception to the race. As such, he should just be content. Brown could not make sense of this perspective and called it "the contradiction of all contradictions."[19] Instead, Brown minced few words in making sure that the public knew that his motivation and accomplishments on the field were distinct from his aspirations after the game. He made it clear that he played the game because he thrived on the competition and loved the financial reward, but that his identity as a black man was a separate subject. Brown played his heart out on the field as he had always done, but he never pretended that rushing for 150 yards or scoring four touchdowns in a game put him on equal footing in the eyes of America.

Brown's sense of context helped him realize that voicing what he viewed as American hypocrisy in the late 1950s would earn him the label of radical. In his words, "Unfortunately, the civil rights movement wasn't in full bloom when I first played pro football. I wanted mine, made no bones about it, people called me militant."[20] Brown was very aware of the general civil unrest by African Americans and respected the efforts of Dr. King as the emerging leader of the movement for equal rights. He also had an astute understanding that King's nonviolent philosophy and strategies were critical to blacks changing their status in the United States. Nevertheless he supported the idea that other methods were necessary for comprehensive change to occur. In his autobiography Brown advocates the approach of labor leader A. Philip Randolph and others who relied on facts and figures more than sentiment to motivate change, but he also expressed support for the more confrontational Black Muslims. Although Randolph was recognized as a spirited and relentless leader stemming from his threat to President Roosevelt to organize a March on Washington in 1941, his tactics for racial justice were at least familiar to most Americans. But Brown's endorsement of Black Muslims was not one that America was comfortable with, especially coming from an athlete.

So how was Brown, with his brash personality and cavalier commentaries able to survive and, perhaps thrive, despite society's discomfort with him? The answer to this question may vary from person to person, but at least two components are required for any perspective: his star quality was good for the game and he displayed an unusual candor. Brown arrived on the National Football League scene during a time when the league was still recovering from its discriminatory practices of the previous two decades. Before the 1930s, the league was willing to sign truly outstanding black players as it was struggling to gain legitimacy and needed standout performers. By the 1930s, however, a combination of factors influenced team owners to institute a "gentlemen's agreement" that banned African American players from 1933 to 1946. The impetus for the disappearance of these players was that a handful of them began to retaliate against the unfair treatment they faced from teammates and against opponents. Team owners were unprepared and unwilling to deal with these "troublemakers" and opted to solve the situation by removing African American players. Their decision gained support because the league was much better organized and on solid footing by this time. Further, as team expansion headed to the South, Jim Crow laws would complicate team travel logistics and risk southern fan support.[21]

Finally, the Cleveland Browns of the All-American Football Conference (AAFC), a newly-established league that competed head-to-head with the National Football League, had the courage to overlook the unwritten rule to ban black players. Brown's head coach and part-owner Paul Brown signed black players Bill Willis and Marion Motley in 1946. Both men proved to be outstanding players, consistently earning All-Pro honors. As important, Willis and Motley displayed tremendous resiliency by ignoring on-and-off-the-field racial incidents. Motley later said "If Willis and I had been anywhere near being hotheads, it would have been another ten years till black men got accepted in pro ball."[22] It should also be noted that after Willis and Motley joined the Browns, the team went on to four consecutive league championships. The Browns enjoyed similar success after the AAFC folded and they joined the NFL in 1951, which got the attention of the other teams in the league. Slowly but surely over the next decade, NFL teams began to consider African American players. The last team to sign a black player, the Washington Redskins, did so in 1962.

Thus when Jim Brown entered the NFL in 1957, a group of African American pioneers had already reintegrated the league. Because of their accomplishment on the field and the teams' successes in filling the seats, all Brown had to do was prove himself on the gridiron. To say that he was a standout would be an understatement. Brown quickly becoming the premier player at his position and dominated the NFL every year in which he played. He started in his first year by winning the Rookie of the Year award, and proceeded to be named to the Pro Bowl for nine consecutive seasons. Because of his star status, people tolerated Brown's outspokenness about his discontent with racism in the game and society at-large.

The other reason why people put up with Brown was that, on some level, they respected his brutal honesty. By the mid-1960s, America had faced numerous battles and confrontations that had forced people to realize the country was in racial disarray. Ranging from nonviolent protests and sit-ins to in-your-face riots and antiwhite sentiment, Americans in all contexts were seeking solutions. The athletic world, however, viewed itself as "ahead of the curve" on racial matters. By this time the three major sports in America, baseball, basketball, and football, had desegregated, giving them a false sense of security that the incidents of the day did not really concern them. Brown reminded them that the distinction many made between sports and society was bogus. For example, he highlighted the disconnect between bringing notoriety to the Browns and the city of Cleveland through his football exploits, but not being allowed to purchase a house that he desired because of its location in a white neighborhood rather than for lack of financial resources.

Although he was one of very few players who was considered too good to dismiss for such a stance, Brown knew that by expressing how he felt about his expectations and those of other black professional football players, he was jeopardizing support from fans, owners, and even teammates. Yet throughout his career he remained committed to discussing sensitive racial issues in a straightforward manner. He proved his commitment to seeking racial change by retiring at the peak of his career, in part to devote more time to race relations. Although he left the game as the NFL's all-time leading rusher, his more important contribution to professional football was using the sport as his platform to fight racism.

When Brown's autobiography was published in 1964, his forthright statements about the country's hypocrisy toward black people shocked many Americans, black and white. A typical reaction by whites was to consider Brown an ingrate who had probably received too much money and attention already. For African Americans who were troubled by Brown's criticisms, they saw him as jeopardizing opportunities for more blacks to join the privileged ranks of professional sports. But compared to another superstar black athlete, Cassius Clay, Jim Brown must have seemed much more moderate than militant.

"I shook up the world" was the phrase shouted repeatedly by boxer Cassius Clay after defeating Sonny Liston on February 26, 1964 to become the heavyweight champion of the world. Indeed, much of the boxing world was still astonished by Clay's victory. Liston was a rugged, veteran fighter, and Clay was a baby-faced, unseasoned professional fighter who looked to many more like a light heavyweight fighter than a heavyweight. Clearly as an 8-to-1 favorite, Liston was seen as the guy who would welcome this brash former Olympic champion to the big-time by physically manhandling him in the ring. The experts could not have been more wrong, as Clay's style and superior boxing ability forced Liston to quit after the sixth round. America could not have been more wrong either if it thought that Clay's "shaking up the world" would be restricted to boxing.

At a press conference the day after winning the title, Clay made the following statement when asked about his affiliation with the Nation of Islam: "I know where I'm going, and I know the truth and I don't have to be what you want me to be. I'm free to be what I want."[23] For those who were still wondering about the extent of Clay's affiliation to the religious group, he along with national leader of the Nation of Islam, Elijah Muhammad, confirmed Clay's membership the next day. When told that Muhammad had announced to a group in Chicago that Clay was a follower of Allah, Clay replied, "That is true, and I am proud of it."[24] These poignant words by Cassius Clay two days after becoming boxing's heavyweight champion left Americans, boxing fans or not, confused and dumbfounded. No doubt many were wondering, how could the holder of one of sports' most prestigious prizes, and one that America prided itself on "owning," join an organization that shunned Christianity and openly criticized whites for perpetuating racial bigotry and hatred?

The country was already concerned about the momentum that the Nation of Islam had gained in recent years, and Clay's affiliation with the religious group would only enhance its growing interest. Unlike the recognized civil rights organizations that attempted change through social and political means, the Nation of Islam was a religion that preached a complete ideological overhaul for blacks. Usually referred to as Black Muslims, these followers of Elijah Muhammad advocated segregation and pointed the finger directly at the evil white man to explain racial oppression in America. Such beliefs caused white America to view Black Muslims as extremists who lived by a doctrine of hate.

Also, the emergence of the Nation of Islam's charismatic minister, Malcolm X, had added to society's concerns. A former hustler and criminal in Harlem, Malcolm galvanized northern blacks to stand up and confront their white enemies rather than practice the nonviolent methods of Dr. King and others. Although Malcolm had recently been reprimanded for inappropriate behavior by Elijah Muhammad, American was aware of his relationship with Clay and presence in Miami at the time of the fight.

Also, on the heels of the March on Washington in the previous year and the pressure on President Johnson to honor President Kennedy's Civil Rights program, 1964 already promised to have enough controversy around racial issues. But on March 6 Clay would validate the country's anxieties by revealing his "new self" to America. On a radio broadcast that evening, Elijah Muhammad announced that professional sports' newest superstar would no longer be called by his "slave name." Instead, he would forever be known as Muhammad Ali.[25]

Although America knew about Ali's relationship with Malcolm X and Ali's presence at Muslim rallies had been publicized, his announcement and name change stunned the nation. Most whites were angry and many blacks felt betrayed. Whites, especially Ali supporters, were annoyed because they overlooked his boisterous style, thinking that there was substance behind it. Blacks labeled him as disloyal for two reasons. First, by converting to Islam he had turned his back on Christianity, the overwhelming religious choice and spiritual foundation for African Americans since the early days of slavery. Perhaps the most glaring example of blacks' contempt was expressed by Ali's father, Cassius Clay, Sr., who spoke out against the Nation of Islam, stating "They have ruined my two boys; they should run those Black Muslims out of this country before they ruin other fine people."[26] Second, the prominence of an African American as the heavyweight champion was a sense of pride for most blacks, and the race needed its champion to represent the race properly. Ali's showmanship and denouncing of Christianity made him frightfully close to the first black heavyweight champion Jack Johnson.

Almost as if he sensed the potential comparisons, Ali tried to dismantle such perceptions claiming, "I am a good boy. I never have done anything wrong. I have never been in jail. I have never been in court. I don't join any integration marches. I don't pay any attention to all those white women who wink at me. I don't carry signs."[27] These words capture the Muhammad Ali that America would learn more about throughout the remainder of the decade. Ironically, they also describe why so many rationalized Ali's conversion to Islam as nothing more than falling prey to Elijah Muhammad's manipulative influence to capitalize on Ali's fame and soon-to-be fortune. American's were for the most part ignorant of the beliefs and practices of Black Muslims, and viewed them only as a radical antiwhite group. And from everything they knew about Muhammad Ali, he did not fit the mean-spirited, disloyal black men who allegedly joined the organization.

Ali was born on January 12, 1942 to Odessa and Cassius Clay, Sr. in the border city of Louisville, Kentucky. Historically, Louisville has been described as a "selectively southern" place. This connotation stems from the city taking pride in its warm hospitality that differentiated the city from Cincinnati, its less friendly rival city to the north. Also, the city was absent of the virulent forms of racial violence so vivid in the history of most southern cities. Louisville was built on industrial and railroad jobs, and black Louisvillians were consistently reminded that by living there they escaped the exploitive agricultural work typically reserved for their counterparts farther south. Still, African Americans in Louisville faced restricted opportunities to earn a living, and they were usually relegated to the dirtiest and lowest paying positions in all industries.

Ali grew up in the community near "Smoketown" where many of the black working class lived. He began boxing at age 12 after some kids stole his bike. In anticipation of crossing their paths, he wanted to be able to defend himself when he took back what belonged to him. His interest and instincts in the sport led to early success. At the young age of 18, Ali won the gold medal at the 1960 Olympics in Rome, Italy. Although already recognized as a cocky fighter by this time, he was able to get away with some of his antics because he had made America proud by his Olympic performance. In the eyes of mainstream America, he was seen as American first and foremost; his identity as black was somewhere down the list. In the coming years the country would learn that in Ali's mind, his African heritage ranked far above his relationship with America.[28]

After defeating Liston and unsettling much of the country with his conversion to Islam and subsequent name change, Ali continued to dominate the heavyweight boxing division. At the same time Ali's popularity, particularly among African Americans, continued to rise. Perhaps a part of his increased status can be attributed to the overall efforts of blacks in changing the racial terrain in America. Although not all blacks supported his detachment from Christianity, they commended the courage to follow his convictions. Throughout the early years of his reign as champion, African Americans continued to pursue their passion for equality by chipping away at the country's unjust practices. Through the courtrooms, public streets and private facilities, blacks challenged the status quo. In 1965, the monumental Voting Rights Act ended the legal exclusion of blacks to voice their rights as citizens. Participation in the political process gave African Americans the foundation in which to make social, political, and economic changes, especially in the South where the majority of blacks resided and where they faced their toughest resistance. Ali's next true fight would not be in the ring; rather, it would be against the American government.

Before 1966, Ali had articulated his opposition to the Vietnam War. As had been the public response to his conversion to Islam, his position was met with mixed reaction. Other outspoken activist shared Ali's perspective on the moral and political criticism of the United States' military involvement, but similar to blacks' response to all American wars in the twentieth century, Vietnam was another chance for blacks to prove their loyalty to the country. But in February 1966, Ali went beyond verbal criticism when he requested deferment from military duty. His request was denied, but in the public's eyes, the damage had been done. Ali had betrayed the country at a time when unconditional support was expected. Proving that it was not a publicity ploy as some assumed, he initiated a legal battle that would last until 1971.

By now it was apparent that the controversy surrounding Ali would be a long and arduous. He ensured that the confrontation was held on the nation's television screens and front pages of its newspapers when he made the dramatic statement, "Man, I ain't got no quarrel with them Viet Cong." Ali revised his rejection of America's military involvement by seeking exemption as a conscientious objector, but again his appeal was denied. With his 1-A military classification upheld, Ali was required to follow through with induction into the military at the appropriate time. When it was time for him to report for induction on April 28, 1967 in Houston, Texas, Ali was there. But as expected, he refused to step forward when instructed. Ali released a statement claiming, "I have searched my conscience and I find I cannot be true to my belief in my religion by accepting such a call."[29]

In the legal reaction to follow, Ali was indicted and found guilty of draft evasion. Of interest, only a few hours after he had refused induction and before he was later indicted, boxing's governing body stripped him of his title and revoked his boxing license. The sport that he had done so much for in such a short period had abandoned him before it was appropriate to do so officially. Ultimately on June 28, 1971, the U.S. Supreme Court would decide on a technicality that Ali's objection to the war was based on legitimate religious reasons. This announcement freed him to resume his boxing career after losing four critical years in his career. But more important than retaining the right to display his remarkable talents to boxing fans, the Court's decision was a signature moment for African American activists' morale. Unquestionably Ali's willingness to tolerate relentless criticism and to forfeit enormous financial reward was commendable. But to do it because of his principles and without seeking solace was inspirational for other freedom fighters. Fellow African American sports icon and activist Bill Russell summed up Ali's influence best: "I envy Muhammad Ali. He has something I have never been able to attain and something very few people I know possess. He has an absolute and sincere faith."[30]

By 1968, Russell, Brown, and Ali were three of the more prominent athletes to join the efforts of scholar and activist Dr. Harry Edwards. In 1967, Edwards began organizing the Olympic Project for Human Rights (OPHR), an initiative to protest the International Olympic Committee's acceptance of apartheid South Africa and the United States' seemingly indifference to treatment of black people in that country. The OPHR pushed hard for African American athletes to consider boycotting the 1968 Olympic Games. The support of Russell, Brown, and Ali, along with other recognized black activists such as King and Stokely Carmichael, added legitimacy to Edwards' plea. A boycott of the Olympics seemed like a real possibility when numerous key black track athletes and teams boycotted the prestigious New York Athletic Club meet in February 1968. The International Olympic Committee (IOC) dismissed the protest and announced that South Africa would still be allowed to compete. The OPHR's stance, however, was a galvanizing force, as other organizations and more than 30 countries joined in support of staying away from the games later that summer. This got the IOC's attention and its chairman, Avery Brundage, instituted a ban on South African participation. This gesture was considered compromise enough for America's black athletes, and they decided to compete and represent the nation. Still, some displayed personal signs of protest, with the most noted being Tommie Smith and John Carlos's infamous moment with heads bowed and fists raised on the medal stand for the 200-meter dash.[31]

Without the initiative of the OPHR and the involvement of Russell, Brown, and Ali in this quest for civil rights, the IOC might have allowed South Africa to participate in the 1968 Olympic Games. Fortunately the situation did not come down to black athletes having to decide whether or not to sacrifice their personal goals for the greater cause. But had they been required to do so, the presence of these three athletes who had proven that they were not afraid to go against mainstream American sentiment would have inspired at least some of the athletes to boycott.

In addition to appreciating their contributions during the Civil Rights movement 40 years ago, it is critical to recognize how each continues to make his mark in society. For example, Russell was a pioneer in breaking barriers for blacks in the coaching and management ranks (the focus of the next chapter); Brown started the Amer-I-Can program, which works with gang members and ex-convicts to help them become positive members in society; Ali has come full circle from his days as representing the country in the 1960 Olympics to lighting the final Olympic torch in the 1996 Olympic games in Atlanta, Georgia. Because of the risks they were willing to take when nobody knew the outcome, and because of their continued participation in social justice long past their playing careers, Bill Russell, Jim Brown, and Muhammad Ali continue to be central figures in the advancement of blacks in sports and in greater society.

4

THE RULES HAVE CHANGED BUT THE GAME IS STILL THE SAME: BLACK ATHLETES' ACHIEVEMENTS IN THE CIVIL RIGHTS ERA AND BEYOND

The numerous situations connected to civil rights, many of which came to a head in some form or fashion in 1968, influenced black athletes and American society years down the road. This chapter illustrates how subsequent years unfolded for African Americans in sport as a lens by which to understand overall racial progress. In doing so, I consider various individuals who had tremendous impact on their particular sport but also forced the United States at large to confront or redress broader issues. Specifically, I analyze the context for significant pioneering developments through Curt Flood and Frank Robinson in baseball, and for football through Doug Williams.

As suggested in the previous chapter, 1968 must be regarded as a benchmark year when discussing the interplay between race and sports in the United States. Perhaps no other event symbolized this more than the Olympic Games of that year in Mexico City. As the primary initiator of Olympic Project of Human Rights (OPHR), scholar and activist Harry Edwards led black athletes in boycotting the New York Athletic Club's prestigious track meet just a few months before the start of the Olympics. Edwards's obvious intentions to follow up the New York Athletic Club boycott with a more comprehensive one in Mexico City was considered an irritation at least and catastrophic at worst by most interested observers. Described as "the revolt of the black athlete," Edwards sought to prove that black athletes were a critical component to the overall black liberation movement and, in some ways, even more important given their national and international platform via the sporting world.[1] Ultimately, most Olympic African American athletes decided to participate in the games rather than have their years of hard work and sacrifice dismissed as a result of lack of participation. Yet the infamous fisted salutes and bowed heads by John Carlos and Tommie Smith on the medal stand of the 200-meter dash reinforced the reality that black athletes in particular and black people in general would not surrender the ultimate fight for equality. The effect of this intentional rejection of inequality was best stated by boycott spokesman Lee Evans, who told a journalist, "A few years ago I didn't know what was happening. My white junior college coach used to tell colored boy jokes and I'd laugh. Now I'd kick his ass."[2]

Evans's embittered comments captured what many African Americans were feeling by the end of one of America's most eventful decades. His comments are noteworthy because he represented the now outspokenly critical black athlete against racial mockery rather than the silent recipient whom whites had come to expect. The passion and resentment in which Evans and others spoke were in response to how the white authority figures who, at least on the surface, were expected to have been above the degradation of blacks. And it was such public display of resentment against the day-to-day and athletic status quo that captured the spirit of standout baseball outfielder, Curt Flood.

Between the end of the 1969 baseball season and the start of the 1970 season, Curt Flood was traded from the St. Louis Cardinals to the Philadelphia Phillies. To get traded from one major league club to another was not unusual; from 1965 to 1970, fewer than half of major league players remained with the same team. Being released or traded was as old as the game itself and deemed merely a characteristic of the business side of baseball. But in Flood's case, he rejected the move from one team to the other. This reaction was startling for several reasons. First, professional baseball players did not have the right-of-refusal in transferring teams; second, Flood was a respected, exceptional player whose pay was in the league's upper echelon; third, he was an African American man questioning the sacred structure of an American institution. For all of these reasons, Flood's decision to stand up against baseball etiquette makes it one of the most profound acts in baseball history. To understand Curt Flood's choice to combat baseball's systems requires insight into Flood the player and person, as well as the broader context in which he played.

Curt Flood's journey to baseball stardom was not predictable. When he signed his first professional contract just out of high school in 1956, there were few players for him to emulate. Despite having shown exceptional athleticism by this time, Flood was a diminutive black kid in what was very much a game for larger white men. Further, Flood already had shown considerable talent as an artist, and his thoughtful, introspective manner was not typically associated with African American athletes of the day.

Flood's upbringing played a prominent role in the principled man that he became. Born in Houston, Texas on January 18, 1938, Flood was the youngest of six children in Herman and Laura Flood's family. The family moved to Oakland, California, seeking a better life when Curt was only a toddler. Curt's parents modeled hard work and decency for their children. Both his mother and father worked at least two jobs during his childhood and taught Curt and his siblings right from wrong in an effort to give them a foundation for a better life. According to Curt, this meant that his parents wanted their children to have a decent job, a loving family, a respectable home, no trouble with the law, and no problem with drinking or drugs.[3] To have parents who sought this for their children was not atypical of African American families in the 1940s and 1950s, but nevertheless it provided an important foundation not to be taken for granted.

Although Flood's parents were not known to be especially active in the Civil Rights movement, in teaching their children such a value system, it is no surprise that Flood became a self-proclaimed "child of the 1960s." He watched his parents work constantly just so they could put food on the table and keep a roof over their heads; in Flood's words, they "ransomed themselves to a vision of the future." Flood's recollection of most of his peers and many in his community was one of "paralyzed indignation," a mindset in which people did their best to make it from one day to the next. On reflection, however, Flood credits Jim Chambers, a white art teacher at Oakland's Herbert Hoover Junior High School, for helping shape his black consciousness at an early age. In training him to appreciate art, Chambers taught Flood that art was not about technique, but a resource of the human spirit. In Flood's words, "He accepted my blackness without fuss. More precisely, he appreciated blackness as a central attribute."[4] Throughout Flood's adult life, his talents as a painter were acknowledged as distinct in the same ways that his talents were on the diamond; but few realized, perhaps not even Flood himself, how prominent art was to his essence as a person. His love of art and appreciation of culture in general became important characteristics that distinguished Flood from the typical baseball player.

Flood signed a $4,000 a year contract with the Cincinnati Reds right out of high school. He received no bonus, but all he was concerned with was a chance at the major leagues. He knew his journey would be difficult. It had only been nine years since his hero, Jackie Robinson, had integrated the major leagues. But he was optimistic about his chances of succeeding, especially since signing with the Reds meant he would rejoin with his high school teammate, Frank Robinson. On arrival at the Reds training camp in Tampa, Flood realized that he had entered a different world than the one he left in Oakland. When he arrived at the hotel where the other players were staying, he noticed the drinking fountains labeled "Colored" and "White." This was his first reminder that he was in a place where Jim Crow laws were still very much the order of the day. What happened next, however, would remind him how firmly entrenched racial segregation was in the South. Flood was under the impression that he would be staying at the hotel with the other Reds players, but when he attempted to check in, he was told that he would be staying at Ma Felder's place. Ma Felder's boardinghouse was where Frank Robinson and the other handful of black players in the Reds organization resided. This powerful dose of reality for Flood, that he was a black man first and baseball player second, would remain with him for his entire playing career.

Flood was assigned to the Reds's Class B High Point-Thomasville minor league team in North Carolina out of spring training. Although being sent there was a compliment in baseball terms in comparison to most first-year ballplayers (most were sent to the class D team), Flood personally faced the rude reality that his baseball abilities could not compensate for his blackness. In his autobiography, *The Way It Is*, he states that "One of my first and most enduring memories is of a large, loud cracker who installed himself and his four little boys in a front-row box and started yelling 'black bastard' at me."[5] In addition to the racial epithets that he heard on the field, Flood was not included as a true member of the team; that is, when his team was not playing a game, Flood was either ignored by his teammates or refused entry into the typical social culture of baseball players.

Based on his game time performance, no one would ever suspect that the blatant disrespect that Flood experienced bothered him during his first year of professional baseball. He appeared to take it all in stride, almost as if he had grown accustomed to such ill treatment, and put up very impressive numbers. Flood played in all 154 games and led the league in batting average (.340), runs batted in (128), and hits (190). And to top it off, he hit 29 home runs, an amazing number for someone who stood 5'7" and barely weighed 140 pounds. But the verbal harassment from folks in the stands, the disregard from his teammates, and the fact that he had no one on his team to help him cope with such humiliating experiences did affect Flood. Early in his first season he would harness much of his frustration until returning to his room at Ma Felder's or its equivalent, where he would burst into tears.

As the season progressed and questions about whether he could compete on the field were erased, Flood not only began to cry less, he began to defend himself and those of his race. In one instance, Flood approached a white teammate before a game about antagonizing a black kid for jumping onto the field and taking a baseball. The ballplayer yelled at the boy, "Hey you black nigger, come back with that ball." He then proceeded to climb into the stands and take the ball from the boy. Flood approached his teammate and told him, "Don't use that word around me. You owe me more respect than that. White kids steal baseballs all the time without interference, you wool-hat son-of-a-bitch. If you ever come near me again you'll be sorry."[6] Such a reaction demonstrates that Flood had had enough.

He, like so many African Americans of the mid to late 1950s, had reached a point where a degree of fundamental respect was required rather than optional. By Flood's first season of professional baseball, important civil rights initiatives emerged that influenced the entire nation. In addition to the *Brown v. Board of Education* decision, the Montgomery bus boycott, Emmitt Till murder, and the desegregation of Little Rock, Arkansas Central High School had taken place. The impetus for these events, especially the latter three, was unequivocal disrespect. In each instance, individuals were violated beyond even the typical lowly status assigned to African Americans of the day. Specifically, when Rosa Parks, a mild-mannered and well-respected black woman in Montgomery, Alabama was arrested for failing to relinquish her bus seat, it represented how inflexible southern racial mores were to even the most nonthreatening individuals. In the case of Till, the physical violence inflicted on a young black boy for simply acknowledging a white woman in a manner deemed unacceptable, and the legal mockery that freed his culprits without punishment, was a blatant devaluing of black people's lives. And in the case of the courageous students and their families who attempted to put into operation what the city of Little Rock, Arkansas had declared permissible, they endured relentless demands by segregationists to maintain the status quo of racially divided schools; so much pressure was exuded to squelch the desegregation of Central High School that the National Guard had to be brought in to protect the black students attending the school.

These events, which became catalysts for efforts in the Civil Rights movement at-large, also influenced individuals such as Curt Flood. He was still very young and was busy trying to prove his worth in the world of baseball, but he also was in the process of making sense of American society and his place as a black man within it. Flood's thoughtful and introspective manner was destined to collide with the rudimentary traditions of baseball much like black Americans' onslaught of challenging racial inequities was the culmination of consistent forms of struggle and protest. Yet unlike most professional black athletes at the time, even those who despised the exploitive nature of their respective sport, Flood never seemed to accept baseball's system of oppression.

In determining what made Flood unique in comparison to ball players of his era, one important distinction about him emerges—by the time he entered professional sports he had already demonstrated exceptional talent in an area removed from athletics. Art, particularly painting, was a passion of Flood's even before baseball. Flood credits art teacher Jim Chambers for helping to cultivate his artistic talent and what it means to be an artist. Flood expressed, "He aroused in me the sensibilities that finally enable a painter to illuminate life instead of merely illustrating it."[7] As important, Chambers introduced Flood to Marian Jorgensen, Chambers's cousin. Marian and her husband, Johnny, would become Flood's second family, and they reassured Flood that the division between blacks and whites in society was not inevitable or necessarily permanent, especially once Flood decided to test baseball's reserve clause.

When Flood was first told that he had been traded in October 1969, he planned to retire in protest. But his good friend Marian Jorgensen encouraged him to challenge baseball's rules. Flood knew that others had been previously unsuccessful in their attempts to overturn the right for baseball teams to trade players at their discretion, but none of those players had been a three-time all star or team captain for four consecutive years in which his team won three pennants and one World Series title. Thus

Flood decided to fight baseball and expose American society to his self-defined "brand of rage."

In many ways Flood's "brand" was similar to the courage and principles that contemporaries such as Muhammad Ali and Jim Brown had displayed. Yet one difference was that baseball was America's game, and any attempt to challenge the sport's sacredness was viewed as a slap in the country's face. Flood's challenge against the ethics of America's pastime was compounded by the fact that as an African American, he was supposed to be more appreciative for the opportunity to participate in the game that many in society still thought of as belonging to whites. Perhaps even more so than his rejection against baseball's archaic policies and procedures, Flood's recognition as an artist challenged the tendency to disregard baseball players away from their performance on the diamond. This was especially true for black players, who typically were acknowledged only for their physical abilities. Flood's renowned artistic expression represented an intellectual acumen and human spirit that contradicted the skills associated with being a great centerfielder or base stealer. These attributes, which distinguished him from even his white baseball counterparts, were shunned by baseball's establishment and society at-large.

Flood rejected such subjective sacredness by sending baseball commissioner Bowie Kuhn a letter on Christmas Eve claiming that he refused to be treated like "a piece of property" and rejected the trade that would send him to Philadelphia against his wishes. Stating that the reserve clause was "a form of indentured slavery," Flood understood that his decision had, in essence, ended his professional baseball career, and that few would support his decision in public regardless of their personal convictions. Although he understood why people supported him no closer than at arms length, he would remain troubled that no active player stepped forward on his behalf. But Flood was a man of his principles who understood, perhaps before anyone else did, that it was his character as much as his acrobatic catches in the outfield that lay at the foundation for why baseball fans, the people of St. Louis, and fellow major league players admired him from 1958 to 1969.

By the late 1970s, baseball had begun to relax some of its rules related to the reserve clause, and players began to exercise the option to market their services and negotiate better contracts with other teams in the major leagues. Despite paving the road for such changes, Flood remained a virtual outcast from baseball until the 1990s. Namely, Ken Burns's "Baseball" documentary and Spike Lee's television feature on Flood recognized him favorably; even the introduction of "The Curt Flood Act" to Congress, which legally ended baseball's antitrust exemption, was a nice gesture. But none of these actions could replace what Flood lost with his decision to challenge baseball's reserve clause: hundreds of thousands of dollars, coaching and managing opportunities, or a legitimate chance at Baseball's Hall of Fame. Yet to Flood, his career was fulfilled in knowing that by remaining true to his principles, baseball would forever be a reflection of what is possible in America rather than just the sport founded there.

When Flood died of inoperable throat cancer in January, 1997, baseball and society had managed to focus on the positives associated with his challenge to baseball's reserve clause before the 1970 season. Yet as the 1970s unfolded, African Americans and black athletes still held tenuous places in American society in general and the sports community in particular. On the one hand, the rebelliousness exuded in the 1960s by black activists and everyday people was paralyzing to the country. On the other hand, the sporting world realized it not only had to deal with black athletes, but that they were necessary to truly captivate a national audience.

The recognition of African American athletes in the 1970s and 1980s occurred in the context of significant changes of black stature in society. Although many of the symbols of social dissent had trickled away, political activism was alive and thriving during the 1970s. Specifically, the political arena was the platform for economic and educational advancement during this era. As evidence of this fact, between 1965 and 1975, the number of blacks elected to public office increased from approximately 100 to more than 3,500 throughout the nation; blacks in the U.S. House of Representative increased from 6 to 17; and the number of black mayors grew from 8 in 1971 to 135 in 1975.[8]

As important as this rise in political representation was the national black movement in which it took place. *Black Power*, the term and philosophy, had taken root in many African American communities across the country. The term was coined in the national sphere during the tumultuous summer of 1966, after the assassination attempt of James Meredith as he began his 200-mile trek from Memphis, Tennessee, to Jackson, Mississippi. Meredith, the same man who four years earlier had broken the color line at the University of Mississippi, was seeking to highlight the institutional racism that continued to dominate much of the South's Delta region by staging a "March Against Fear." Viewed as outside agitators by the white press and locals, the Civil Rights group leadership and members such as King and Southern Christian Leadership Conference, Floyd McKissick and the Congress of Racial Equality, and Stokely Carmichael of the Student Non-Violent Coordinating Committee (SNCC), came together in unity to finish Meredith's effort to bring national attention to the racial violence and arrogance that persisted in the South.[9]

Carmichael, the brash young leader of SNCC, had attracted a significant following who wanted to push the envelope beyond the traditional, interracial, and nonviolent approach to achieving racial justice. Instead, Carmichael declared that black people wanted to define progress by their own terms rather than being told that society was changing and things were getting better for them. And in his words, "the only way we gonna stop them white men from whuppin' us is to take over. We been saying freedom for six years and we ain't got nothin'. What we gonna start saying now is Black Power!"[10] This assertion got the country's attention as the national media validated people's fears and concerns that racial combat was a real possibility.

Despite the uncritical reaction to the term Black Power as a call to arms, there was a fundamental philosophy behind the words. In essence, Black Power demanded that African Americans be taken seriously. Certainly this included social equality, but just as important, it also included a real and legitimate opportunity to have a stake in America's economic and political culture. Further, it required a recognition and appreciation of blacks as culturally distinctive from the country's racial majority.

Although a methodical process would be required before these goals would be achieved, the big three professional sports witnessed several symbolic developments to suggest that change was possible during the Black Power era of 1965–75. In basketball, the first was Bill Russell being named player-coach of the Boston Celtics in 1966. As previously discussed, the opportunity for Russell, an outspoken and principled man, to succeed legendary coach Red Auerbach and lead the famed Boston Celtics was a monumental breakthrough for African American athletes. Until Russell, star black athletes were never considered as legitimate candidates for coaching or executive positions for professional sports franchises, regardless of demonstrated ability in their particular sport or their understanding of the intricacies of the game. In baseball, the hiring of Frank Robinson as manager of the Cleveland Indians in 1975, 30 years after Jackie Robinson broke the color barrier, was a monumental achievement. In football, the hiring of Art Shell as head coach would not come until 1989.

As the oldest professional sports league in this country and "America's pastime," baseball has embodied this presumed practice of blacks as the performers and whites as decision makers since the sport's earliest days. As has been well documented, baseball's whites-only clause instigated the formation of a separate major leagues for African Americans. From the talent scouts who followed them regularly to the occasional fan of the exhibition games between major and Negro leaguers, it became quite apparent over the years that blacks playing in the Negro leagues possessed the skills and insight into the game to perform at least on par with their counterparts in the major leagues. Yet the commitment to racial segregation between the two leagues essentially ensured black ball-players' second-class status. At best, the star Negro leaguers would be granted "asterisk status," which basically meant that baseball fans would always be reminded that their records and performances occurred in the Negro leagues. Such labeling, whether or not intentional, guarantees questioning of the legitimacy of the league and those who were part of it.

When major league baseball could no longer ignore such a rich talent pool of baseball prospects, it desegregated with the signing of Jackie Robinson to a minor league contract in 1945. Robinson reached the major leagues in 1947, and teams began to slowly allow more black players to join their organizations and parent clubs. Despite the gradual inclusion of African Americans to the major leagues, thinking of these players beyond their on-the-field contributions was not yet on the minds of the baseball establishment. Throughout the 1950s, teams were still in the process of including even one or two black players on the major league roster, often making sure that they found the right blend of talent and personality so as to not upset the either the white players or, more important, the paying customers. The 1960s saw a constant increase in the number of African American and Latin ballplayers, but most of these players realized how tenuous their positions were with their respective teams. They understood that organizations were unlikely to field a team that had too many non-white players. Thus if you were a black or Latin player, earning a starting position and clearly outperforming your white competition was the only way you could have confidence that you would not be sent back to the minor leagues, traded or released.

Beginning in the mid-1950s, Frank Robinson became one of those few African American players whose undeniable talent forced baseball to reserve a spot for him. Robinson signed a professional contract that included a $3,500 bonus with the Cincinnati Reds in 1953. He had starred at McClymonds High School in Oakland, the same school that produced basketball great Bill Russell and baseball standout Curt Flood, before signing with the Reds. Robinson rose quickly through the Reds's system, making his major league debut as the starting right fielder at the beginning of the 1956 season. Robinson had a tremendous first season and won the National League's Rookie of the Year award. This was the beginning of an outstanding playing career that lasted 20 years. Throughout his tenure in the major leagues, Robinson was a 13-time all-star, winner of the triple crown in 1966, and the recipient of the Most Valuable Player award in both the National and American leagues, the only major leaguer in history to win this award in both leagues. Robinson's accolades for his accomplishments on the field reached baseball's pinnacle when he was voted into the sports Hall of Fame in 1982.[11]

Despite the success he and his teams enjoyed on the baseball diamond, Robinson's most significant contribution to the game may have been when he was named player-manager of the Cleveland Indians in 1974 for the 1975 season. When the Indians acquired Robinson late in the 1974, rumors began circulating that Robinson could possibly be named the team's manager for the next season. This suggestion was dismissed as rumor by many in baseball, as well as those who followed the game. Certainly the major leagues had evolved to the point where black players were prominent in the game, but there was no serious track record of an African American being considered for a major league manager's position. Yet a closer look at Robinson beyond his performance on the field suggested that he had other plans. Even early in his career in Cincinnati, Robinson was recognized as a team leader. Nicknamed "The Judge," this fiery player with a competitive spirit was known to call team meetings to motivate his teammates to play to their potential. As a leader with both the Cincinnati Reds and the Baltimore Orioles, where he was traded before the 1966 season, Robinson and his teammates played in five World Series championships, twice winning the title with Baltimore. To those who bothered to take notice, Robinson was preparing to manage in the major leagues before his playing days ended. In the early 1970s, he spent

his off-seasons managing winter ball to gain some experience in anticipation of receiving an opportunity to break the barrier that no other black
had before him.[12]

Finally, at the end of the 1974 season, the Cleveland Indians made
baseball history by announcing that Robinson would take the helm as the
team's manager for the 1975 season. He would also continue as a player.
At the press conference announcing his hiring, Robinson demonstrated
his understanding of the significance of becoming baseball's first African
American manager. Although not known as the sentimental type,
Robinson made the statement, "If I had one wish in the world today, it
would be that Jackie Robinson could be here to see this happen."[13] This
reflection helped baseball and society at-large place in context the
significance of this decision.

Of course not everyone was thrilled with the decision. Almost 30 years
had elapsed since the major leagues had desegregated. Relinquishing the
power and control instilled in a manager was no small feat. Even some of
the Indians' players questioned the decision. One in particular, pitcher
Gaylord Perry, was outspoken about his uncertainty about Robinson's
ability to lead the team. Perry, a southerner who would eventually join
Robinson in the Hall of Fame, shared the concerns held privately by many
others. There may have been other reasons for apprehension, but Perry
and others were certainly conscious of Robinson's reputation as confrontational both on and off the field.

Throughout his playing career, Robinson was known to stand extremely
close to the plate while in the batter's box, almost as if he was daring
pitchers to throw the ball close to him. This strategy worked for him, as
he did not mind getting hit by a pitch thrown too far inside (he set the
rookie record of being hit by a pitch 20 times in 1956) and, if a pitcher left
the ball out over the plate, Robinson would usually deposit it in the stands
behind the outfielders for a homerun. He was also an aggressive base run-
ner who did not avoid collisions on the base paths. The most noted of his
collisions occurred in 1959, when he slid hard into Atlanta Braves third
baseman and superstar Eddie Matthews. Robinson's actions led to an
intense brawl between him and Matthews, the first of its kind between an
African American and white superstar.[14] Perhaps most striking is that the
incident took place in Atlanta, Georgia, the place still recognized by
many at the time as the capital of Dixie, where segregation and racial
disparity remained the practice and rule. Robinson was booed loudly and

undoubtedly heard jeers after this incident, but he responded by hitting a grand slam the next opportunity he had against the Braves.

During this same time period, when the Civil Rights movement was growing in national support and intensity, Robinson also became more assertive in responding to personal threats. He began carrying a gun in self-defense after several death threats, and was arrested for flaunting it in a restaurant when he was refused service. In another incident after he was traded to Baltimore, Robinson spoke out on behalf of the local National Association for the Advancement of Colored People's protest against the segregated housing practices and discrimination in the city's real estate business.

Thus, the combination of a no-nonsense approach to baseball and his willingness to publicly defy racial injustice made Robinson an uncomfortable choice for many as the first African American to manage in the major leagues. Still, on April 8, 1975, Robinson took the field as player-manager for the Cleveland Indians. A fitting tribute to this special moment was made by Rachel Robinson, widow of Jackie, throwing out the ceremonial first pitch. Robinson added even more flare to the occasion by homering in his first at bat during a 5–3 victory over the New York Yankees. Ironically, Gaylord Perry was the winning pitcher for the Indians.[15]

Understanding why Frank Robinson was chosen as baseball's first black manager is no easy task. Certainly he demonstrated that he had the passion and skills to stand out once on the field, but there were others who had come before him who were comparable or better players. Explaining why Robinson was a pioneer in baseball must include the fact that he was not afraid to be unpopular among any group of people. This has served him well throughout his playing and managing career and has much to do with his continued prominence in the game today. After being fired as manager of the Indians in 1977, he managed the San Francisco Giants from 1981 to 1984, the Baltimore Orioles from 1988 to 1991, and has managed the Montreal Expos/Washington Nationals since 2002.[16] He has always seemed unconcerned about whether people agreed with him and still fights for what he believes is right. Ultimately, people respect him for his honesty and for standing behind his convictions.

Perhaps the best example of Frank Robinson's style was his commentary after Al Campanis's 1987 remarks questioning blacks' abilities to hold management positions in baseball. In this famous interview on national television, Campanis, who was an executive with the Los Angeles

Dodgers, essentially regressed to the historical argument that African Americans had the physical skills to excel in athletics but lacked the mental capacities to effectively participate in the business of owning and managing sports franchises. Campanis was fired by the Dodgers and, for all practical purposes, shunned from the baseball world. For many, Campanis received the treatment he deserved for such comments. But rather than focus on Campanis the individual, Robinson reacted to the realities of baseball's closed system for blacks seeking management positions in baseball. Robinson stated that Campanis's "statements are the most significant thing that has happened for blacks in baseball for a long, long time" because it "made people finally understand what goes on behind closed doors."[17] Robinson's assessment may have been difficult for some to hear, but it was much like his response to the question of why he took the managerial job for so many struggling teams: "somebody had to break down the barrier and keep a black man visible."[18]

As stated previously, the racial tumult of 1968 was widespread. The nation's crisis-like atmosphere included events such as the assassination of the Civil Rights movement's most noted leader, Dr. Martin Luther King, Jr., and extended to the international athletic spectacle against America's racist society by African American track and field stars, which shamed the country as they received their Olympic medals. Yet it was also in 1968 when African American athletes began to receive a different level of national notoriety. That year, Arthur Ashe became the first black to win the U.S. Open tennis tournament, Bill Russell was *Sports Illustrated* Sportsman of the Year, and Orenthal James (O.J.) Simpson was named the Heisman Trophy winner and International College Athlete of the Year. This amount of recognition for African American athletes was quite impressive, but not enough to totally overshadow the social, political, and racial clashes at the time.

These tensions seemed to at least raise the consciousness of professional basketball and baseball, but football lagged behind in its efforts to break with tradition. Specifically, football did not name its first African American coach, Art Shell with the Oakland Raiders, until 1989—more than two decades after Russell was named coach of the Boston Celtics and 14 years after Robinson took over as manager of the Cleveland Indians. On the surface it is not apparent why football took so much longer. If, for example, we take a snapshot of the status of each league in 1975, football was not noticeably behind in its proportion of African American players.

By this time there were well over 400 blacks, or approximately 40 percent, on National Football League (NFL) rosters. This percentage was higher than the number in baseball, and although fewer than the number in the National Basketball Association, that league was under scrutiny for being "too black." While each of these leagues was an easy target for its lack of potential head coaches or managers in the pipeline, the NFL could hold its head pretty high for its black player representation in the mid-1970s.

But the NFL did have one glaring eyesore among its racial representation—the dismally low number of African Americans at the quarterback position. In 1975, the league had only one starting quarterback and one other as a backup. These virtually nonexistent figures suggest that there must not have been any legitimate candidates to play this position. Yet when looking at the successful college programs that served as the feeder system to NFL teams, several were led by standout black quarterbacks. By investigating the phenomenon of why these black college quarterbacks were not among the candidates for quarterbacking NFL teams, one can see the seeds for the league's reluctance to hire an African American head coach.

By the 1970s, the quarterback position had been well established as the premier position on the team. Even if a team had dominant defense or an outstanding running back, who the quarterback was and whether or not he could lead the team effectively and efficiently were thought to be determining factors as to the success or failure of a team. In essence, the quarterback was thought of as an extension of the head coach on the field. Not surprisingly, African Americans received little consideration for this position given its image and alleged importance to the team. As journalist Phil Petrie pointed out, even great quarterbacks in the 1950s such as Wilburn Hollis, an All-American leader of the University of Iowa team that finished the season number one in the nation, were not even drafted by the NFL.[19] For countless black quarterbacks who were drafted, they were immediately moved to running back, wide receiver, or defensive back. Occasionally these guys opted to play in the Canadian Football League and later the now defunct World Football League if they were determined to remain as quarterbacks.

The first African American to play quarterback in the NFL was Marlin Briscoe in 1968. Nicknamed "The Magician" because of his skill with the football, Briscoe backed into the job with the Denver Broncos when their starter was hurt and the backups were deemed unacceptable.

Brisco performed wonderfully the remainder of the Broncos season, giving him reason to think that he would retain the job the next year. Surprisingly, Brisco was cut from the Broncos and picked up by the Miami Dolphins, who placed him at wide receiver without ever considering for quarterback. Brisco, like so many other black quarterbacks, had to either swallow this humbling pill and play another position or face the reality that their days in the league would be numbered if they insisted on playing the position they knew so well. For the remainder of the 1960s and much of the 1970s, a few black quarterbacks such as black college stars James Harris from Grambling and Joe Gilliam from Tennessee State University had a moment in the quarterback spotlight, but each was temporary until a white candidate with any promise was handed the job.[20]

The unspoken but deep-rooted taboo of playing a black quarterback in the NFL began to show its first signs of changing when the newly established Tampa Bay Buccaneers drafted Doug Williams in the first round of the 1978 draft. Williams, who had also starred at Grambling, was the first quarterback chosen in the draft that year. Despite this honor, Williams had to hold out of training camp for a week to get a contract worth approximately half of what many other first round selections received in 1978. But Williams was too good for Tampa Bay not to draft early and sign to a multiyear contract. They did not have the luxury of being picky. They were a new franchise that had won only two games in two years. Plus, Williams's talent was undeniable. He was big and strong and possessed arm strength rarely seen. Still, the organization received much scrutiny for their draft selection, with many questioning whether Williams could make the leap to the NFL after allegedly playing against inferior competition among the historically black colleges and universities. No one seemed to recall that, at the time, Grambling had sent more players to the NFL than any other small college and was second only to Notre Dame in total number of players drafted by the NFL.[21]

But the other reason people questioned Williams was less talked about—he did not fit the public image of who would be the first black quarterback to spend his entire NFL career at the position. Williams had several strikes against him that had nothing to do with ability or performance on the football field. In addition to coming from a historically black college, he was quiet, private, and did not go out of his way to make the media or public comfortable with him. He simply wanted to play the game to the best of his abilities and go on about his own business.

These characteristics, combined with being African American, proved for a difficult, albeit excellent, professional career. People did not speak on this issue often outside of closed doors because it was much harder to articulate. How do you say, "Well, Doug Williams had a great year and has helped the Buccaneers grow as a team, but he's not the type of guy my friends and I want to spend time with." But the evidence is there for why Williams never really became a household name in most football circles, beyond the fact that he was a black quarterback. All one has to do is consider that the NFL had set precedent for granting celebrity status on a few black players before they were even proven successes on the professional level, and the other is that Williams received no significant advertising endorsements after leading the Washington Redskins to a Super Bowl victory in 1988 and winning the game's most valuable player award.

The best example of a black player getting carte blanc treatment from the NFL media and football public was Orenthal James (O. J.) Simpson. Simpson's sudden emergence on the national scene as a star running back for the University of Southern California Trojans and his unprecedented popularity in professional football throughout the 1970s made an indelible mark on the NFL. In addition to his exceptional ability on the field, Simpson's charisma, affable manner, and disassociation with racial issues during a particularly difficult racial era made him an instant favorite in most of America. An important reason why Simpson accomplished this status was his insistence that his race be removed from how people saw him. As early as 1969, his rookie year in the NFL, Simpson told reporters with enthusiasm that the American public viewed him as "colorless."[22] Also, he strayed far from endorsing political candidates or commenting on hotly debated political issues, especially if they had racial connotations. And if he happened to speak out on a delicate topic, like he did in the mid-1970s on the absence of black quarterbacks in the NFL, he was sure to speak in support of the league. In this case, he suggested that the oft-injured and aging Joe Namath was a better quarterback for the Los Angeles Rams than his former teammate, black quarterback James Harris. Thus, it is not surprising to learn that in 1976, after Simpson signed the most lucrative contract in the history of the NFL, he was still considered the most admired person in the country by American youth and was football's leading gate attraction.[23] Simpson's strategic approach to his public image combined with success on the gridiron made him the model that other black players, including Doug Williams, would have to emulate to reach Simpson's stature.

By the time Williams won the Most Valuable Player (MVP) award for the Super Bowl, it was understood that the star of that game would be inundated with advertisement and endorsement deals. And if that person happened to be a quarterback as well, he could virtually name his price to interested corporations. After Williams won this award in 1988, everyone began to talk about how much money and notoriety he would receive. After all, Phil Simms, the most recent quarterback who was Super Bowl MVP, had earned about $2 million. Yet for Williams, these opportunities never came. He reported that the only serious offer he considered was from Coca-Cola for $375,000 over three years. But even this offer was for appearance fees only rather than advertisements.[24] Many were shocked to hear about this virtual media disregard for the Super Bowl MVP, but Williams explained that he really was not surprised. He understood that he was not what the public wanted and, just as important, he seemed to be more comfortable with the public's discomfort than they were themselves. In his autobiography, Williams reported, "I was not what they wanted to represent their corporations. That's one thing I've never had a problem with."[25]

Curt Flood, Frank Robinson, and Doug Williams all understood what they were up against in their respective sports. Each of these exceptional professional athletes was an astute observer of the American culture in which they performed their craft. Although Flood, Robinson, and Williams could have taken a more traditional path and perhaps been more celebrated in their era, they would have risked sacrificing the important foundation each laid for today's professional athletes and coaches.

5

"SHE'S DONE MORE FOR HER COUNTRY THAN WHAT THE U.S. COULD HAVE PAID HER FOR": AFRICAN AMERICAN WOMEN AND SPORTS

In 1851, in the small town of Akron, Ohio, Sojourner Truth took her turn on the stage to give her speech at the Women's Rights convention. Although she was greeted rather unpleasantly with boos and hisses, Truth seemed undisturbed and quite focused on making the points that she had come to deliver. In fact, this illiterate, itinerant ex-slave demonstrated unwavering poise as she began by saying:

> Well, chilern, whar dar is so much racket der must be something out of kilter. I tink dat 'twixt de niggers of de Souf and de women at de Norf all a talking' 'bout rights, de white men will be in a fix pretty soon.[1]

Truth went on in her speech to share a few personal experiences that captured the disrespect and disdain that was protocol for how African Americans women experienced life. In each example, Truth, in her improper but articulate speak, asked the question, "and ar'n't I a woman?"[2] Truth's genius, courage, and pioneering spirit made her the first recognized African American woman suffragist. As well, Truth's speech publicized the nonsensical and hypocritical norms of the United States' white, male-dominated culture. As has been demonstrated, American culture has had tremendous impact on the mores in the sporting world. Thus, looking through the lens of sports at how such simple words spoken by Sojourner Truth in the mid-nineteenth century rang true then and continue to have relevance today is the focus of this particular chapter.

Although there has been a significant increase in the amount and quality of scholarship on black women athletes in the last 10 to 15 years, it is still described most accurately as a trickle rather than an outpouring. This is due to several factors—historical limitations of access to sports for women, negative stereotypes assigned to women who participate in certain sports, and the predominance of white male scholars who, unintentionally or not, have given minimal attention to the combination of race (black) and gender (women) in their analyses. In their impressive and important article, "More Myth than History: American Culture and Representations of the Black Female's Athletic Ability," Patricia Vertinsky and Gwendolyn Captain elaborate on how these factors have combined to cause the lag behind in our understanding of African American female athletes' personal experiences, as well as their unique contributions to sports culture.[3] This chapter only nibbles at Vertinsky and Captain's insightful observations, by establishing the "place" of black women in a historical context, and considering important individuals (Wilma Rudolph, Lusia Harris, and Venus and Serena Williams) in a variety of sports (track and field, basketball and tennis), but it hopes to take a small step to complete the picture of interplay between American sports and societal culture.

To look at African American women through a historical lens is to look at a story of struggle. From their incomparable roles in the antebellum South when slavery was the rule, to their oft-shackled activism during the Civil Rights movement, black women have endured a legacy unfamiliar to any other group in American history. To get a clearer understanding of this long-lasting inequity and degradation, it is worth taking a glimpse of African American women in three general periods—the era of slavery, post-slavery to the 1950s, and 1950s through the modern day Civil Rights movement and beyond. When looking at black women athletes against this backdrop, their accomplishments and achievements become even more impressive than the individuals whom I will highlight in this chapter.

Black in a white society, slave in a free society, and woman in a society ruled by men is a crass but meaningful description articulated by historian Deborah Gray White and others to explain what life was like for slave women.[4] Certainly this description reveals the vulnerability inherent in the experiences of slave women. Only within the last 20 years in slavery literature, beginning with White's *Ar'n't I a Woman?*, has it become

explicit that slave women may have experienced that institution's dominance differently than did their male counterparts. Thus there is still more
to learn about the nuances of slave life from the women's perspective. But
what we do know is that slave women were not excused from the complex
roles that were defined later. That is, tension existed between being
viewed as equal yet distinctive from men.

The commitment to the institution of slavery and the wealth that was
at stake prohibited slave owners from caring too much about the slave
women's femininity. Rather, slave women were chattel just like slave men,
and they were expected to work as hard and produce as much as slave
men. Yet the inconsistency in the actions of slave masters confirmed that
slave women had separate and additional roles than did their male counterparts. Specifically, as slave girls reached puberty, their reproductive
capabilities became real to slave masters, for business sake and, at times,
for personal pleasure. As some masters understood the long-term economic consequences of increasing the number of slaves they owned
through reproduction, at least as many viewed these emerging women as
nonromantic places to fulfill their sexual desires.

During this same period in a slave woman's life, the expectations of her
role in the slave quarters or "beyond the master's eye" begin to change as
well. As such, it was incumbent on slave women to assume many of the
gendered expectations of a wife, mother, and household caregiver. Slave
women's ability to alternate between their primary status as a productive
unit in the slavery enterprise and as female beings with different expectations in their personal lives would become the foundation that African
American women athletes would mirror in the postbellum era and
beyond.

Without question, the realities of freedom after the Emancipation Proc-
lamation and end of the Civil War in the 1860s were a work-in-progress,
but the strength and versatility exuded by African American women during slavery were extended once legalized freedom was instituted. Under
the thumb of slavery, most black women, slave and free, remained obscure
in the efforts to challenge and resist racial and sexual inequalities. With
some opportunity to spread their wings, black women began to speak up
and speak out more in the public sphere.

One of the venues where African American women voices were heard
was in the push for suffrage. Before the 1870s, with a few exceptions such
as Sojourner Truth, black women were restricted in their roles in the

fight for women's voting rights. But as pointed out by scholar Rosalyn Terborg-Penn, by the 1870–80s, black women's arguments for the right to vote took on an emphasis specific to women of color.[5] Such an initiative by African American women, which should be thought of as a precursor to the voting rights' efforts of the 1960s, reflects the political awareness and activist spirit that would continue to manifest in the twentieth century.

The primary way in which African American women asserted themselves as change agents was through the formation of social clubs. One of the oldest and most distinguished was the National Association of Colored Women (NACW). During the early years of the twentieth century, the NACW's leadership was instrumental in the formation of National Association for the Advancement of Colored People (NAACP), the premier civil rights organization in the first half of the twentieth century. And, it was many of these women leaders who trained and influenced prominent men leaders like Asa Philip Randolph, whose threat to March on Washington is considered to be the catalyst to the modern Civil Rights movement. Although usually still remaining in the background to the male leadership, at least for public recognition purposes, black women had clearly emerged as significant and necessary components to solving the racial and gender justice problem in the United States.

Also during the early twentieth century, a few important black sporting organizations were founded, in particular, the Colored Intercollegiate Athletic Association (1912), the American Tennis Association (1916), Negro National League (1926), and the United Golfers Association (1926). The Colored Intercollegiate Athletic Association was significant because it provided structure to black colleges and universities athletic programs and provided a camaraderie and unity that helped catapult black college sports after World War I. This organization was especially critical for black college women's participation, as many schools began supporting their women in athletics by the 1930s.

Track and field and basketball were deemed acceptable sports for women by black colleges and universities. Tuskegee Institute, the school founded by Booker T. Washington in 1881, began its women's track and field team in 1929, and the team quickly became recognized for its high-quality performances. The school took a significant step to adding to the team's legitimacy by immediately including them in the Tuskegee Relays, the first major track meet sponsored by a black college. As Susan Cahn points out in her book,

Coming on Strong, allowing women to participate in a meet as significant as the Tuskegee Relays was quickly parlayed into track and field scholarships at Tuskegee and several other black colleges and universities.[6] Thus, during the next decade, black women tracksters from these schools became the backbone for the country's international female track teams, and by the time the Olympic Games resumed in 1948 after World War II cancelled the 1936 and 1940 Games, African American women held 9 of the 11 slots on the track and field team.[7]

To no surprise, the Tuskegee Tigerettes, as they were named, was the premier women's track and field program during the 1930s-40s, winning 11 of 12 Amateur Athletic Union (AAU) championships during this period. Although the Tuskegee teams had fallen on difficult times by the early 1950s, their program had spurred other black schools to develop impressive women's programs that brought accolades to their respective institutions. The next program that emerged to the forefront in the 1950s was at Tennessee State University. The impetus for their success was influenced significantly by Tuskegee Institute's program as Jessie Abbott, the daughter of Tuskegee coach Cleveland Abbott, had established a permanent program at Tennessee State University in 1945.

By the early 1950s, Tennessee State was coached by Ed Temple, who would become one of the most successful women's track and field coaches of the twentieth century. Under the tutelage of Coach Temple, the Tennessee State Tigerbelles produced a phenomenal number of world-class track stars. Tracksters such as Shirley Crowder (Meadows), Martha Hudson (Pennyman), Willye White, Audrey Patterson, Mae Faggs, and Emma Reed excelled in the sport and represented the United States as Olympians. But the most famous Tigerbelle of them all was Wilma Glodean Rudolph.

Rudolph's athletic exploits are legendary—as a high school basketball star she set state scoring records and led her team to a state championship; she won a bronze medal as a 16-year-old in the 1956 Olympic Games; and, in the 1960 Olympic Games she became the first woman to earn three goal medals, winning the 100 and 200 meter dashes and running the anchor for the 400-meter relay team. These noteworthy accomplishments deserve to live forever in track and field lore. As important, Rudolph's story of personal triumph and what she represented to black women in particular, helps to capture the cultural mores that they have had to continually strive to overcome.

Born in Clarksville, Tennessee, in 1940, to Ed and Blanche Rudolph, Wilma faced tremendous obstacles from the beginning of her life. First, although her father had very respectable work as a railroad porter and a mother who worked as caretaker for wealthy white families, Wilma's family was quite poor. Their poverty was due largely to their enormous family. As well, Wilma was one of the youngest (Wilma was the twentieth of 22 children that Ed fathered) of the Rudolph children, so she learned early how to work for whatever she got. Wilma had the additional misfortune of illness and physical problems. Born premature and weighing only 4.5 pounds, Wilma was bedridden much of her early years with double pneumonia, scarlet fever, and polio. Contracting polio caused Wilma to lose the usage of her left leg and forced her to wear a leg brace for the next three years. Wilma clearly got her perseverance and determination from her mother, who for two years traveled to Meharry hospital in Nashville twice a week for treatment on young Wilma's leg. Wilma's mother made this 100-mile round trip by bus consistently with the hope that her daughter would one day walk unassisted. This extensive journey to Meharry was necessary because the local hospital abided by the rules of Jim Crow, which meant that it was for whites only.[8]

Between her mother's heroic efforts and the assistance of her siblings providing the numerous leg rubs required each day to help Wilma improve, she was out of her leg brace by age nine. Wilma's tremendous energy and desire to be like the rest of the kids allowed her to catch up quickly, and by age 12 she was walking normally without even the aid of corrective shoes. It is around this time that her interest in becoming an athlete had a chance to surface.[9]

Of interest, it was starring in her first love of basketball on the girl's team at Burt High School that Rudolph's athletic talents shined initially. Although she was recognized for her ability to score points (she set a state record with 49 points in one game), Rudolph's blazing speed caught the eye of her coach, who also doubled as the Burt High School track coach. Thus when Coach Temple invited Burt High School's track team to Nashville to participate in a meet, the basketball-fast Rudolph was on the team. Rudolph was the star of the meet, winning the 50-, 75-, and 100-yard dashes. Her natural speed caught the eye of Coach Temple, who was working vigorously to establish a pipeline of young talent who could step in and build on the quickly emerging Tigerbelle tradition. Rudolph's work ethic and talent led to a scholarship to Tennessee State University, where she reached unparalleled heights as a nationally and internationally crowned champion. Yet if one looks beyond the numerous trophies and medals she adorned, which admittedly is difficult to do, Rudolph's contribution as a liaison between the races, as well as within the race helped open doors for African American women athletes who followed her.

When Rudolph became the first American women to win three gold medals in the 1960 Olympic Games in Rome, Italy, she also won worldwide adoration. Certainly her standout athletic feats would garner attention, but the fame and adulation that Wilma received had as much to do with how she was regarded off the running surface as much as on it. When speaking about Rudolph after her untimely death in 1994, fellow Olympic teammate Bill Mulliken described her in the following way: "She was beautiful, she was nice, and she was the best."[10] In 1960, holding all of these qualities separated Rudolph from how African American women track and field stars had been perceived previously. Susan Cahn and others have pointed out how white and black communities were critical of extremely athletic women, particularly in track and field, often claiming that they lacked the feminine qualities that fit the most important roles of wife and mother.[11] But Rudolph, facilitated by the interest of Coach Temple, discredited this notion; she was hard-charging and extremely competitive on the track but charming, graceful, and ladylike once the race was over. Because of the restrictive societal expectations and gender roles at that time, being perceived in this regard gave Rudolph the credibility to inspire future women athletes in general and African American ones in particular.

Rudolph's appearance, style, and demeanor were critical to her ability to effect change, even in the context of civil unrest activity brought about by the Civil Rights movement. In 1960, the movement was still very male–dominated, with women typically relegated to background roles. Even in the Montgomery bus boycott, the most famous situation with women at the center up to that point, the national story eventually became the emergence of Dr. Martin Luther King Jr. and his nonviolent resistance strategy. To be sure, Rosa Parks, the Women's Political Council, and the countless black women who refused to ride the bus for an entire year were instrumental, but once the Montgomery Improvement Association was established and subsequently the Southern Christian Leadership Conference was founded in 1957, women were absent from the forefront. Yet like Mrs. Parks and others, Rudolph managed to display strength and conviction while working within the established male hierarchy. Rudolph's decision to work within the acceptable boundaries made possible numerous awards after the Olympics, including the United Press Athlete of the Year (1960), Associated Press Women Athlete of the Year (1960), Columbus Award for Most Outstanding International Sports Personality (1960), and Sullivan Award for Good Sportsmanship (1961) to name a few. Later, she was inducted into the Black Sports Hall of Fame (1980), U.S. Olympic Hall of Fame (1983), and National Women's Hall of Fame (1994).

The best example of Rudolph's contribution in the area of civil rights was her refusal to participate in the hometown festivities planned in her honor unless they were integrated. This was a significant request, as Clarksville, Tennessee, like many places in the South, was accustomed to public racial segregation. All necessary parties agreed to her wishes, recognizing that they could not be outdone by the national and international commendation Rudolph had already received. Rudolph's parade and banquet were reportedly the first integrated events in the town of Clarksville.[12] Further, she also participated in later protests against segregation in Clarksville so that her integrated events could one day, at least legally, become the rule rather than the exception. Rudolph's personal story of overcoming tremendous physical problems, relentless pursuit to be the best and quiet but powerful effort to help change social customs in the area of racial justice continue to motivate and inspire African American women athletes. To Jackie Joyner-Kersee, holder of six Olympic medals, Rudolph was a mentor who "was always in my corner."[13] Her coach, Ed Temple, captured Rudolph's contributions best when he said, "She's done more for her country than what the U.S. could have paid her for."[14]

Rudolph's success in the Olympic Games and willingness to capitalize on her fame to fight racial segregation could not have come at a better time, as the 1960s would become the pinnacle for the Civil Rights movement. For African American women specifically, their leadership roles and prominence would reach unprecedented heights. Two women who set the tone for black women's prominence in leading the movement were Mrs. Ella Baker and Mrs. Fannie Lou Hamer. Although these ladies had come from different backgrounds, they would symbolize the strong-willed and committed black women activist that defined the decade. Mrs. Baker, known for her longtime civil rights work, was college educated (valedictorian at Shaw University in 1927) and accustomed to working closely with prominent leaders such as Dr. Martin Luther King Jr.[15] Mrs. Hamer, on the other hand, was the twentieth child of a Mississippi sharecropper who had little formal education.[16] In an eloquence of their own, they displayed a strength and wisdom that galvanized black people to say "enough is enough" to the racial oppression they had experienced for too long.

No place needed the incomparable leadership of Baker and Hamer more in the early to mid-1960s than the Mississippi Delta. This northwestern quadrant of Mississippi, which extends approximately 200 miles from Memphis, Tennessee to Vicksburg, Mississippi, was the quintessential place for anyone nostalgic about the Old South. Containing some of the most fertile soil, this region still grew a disproportionate amount of the nation's cotton and had a majority black population. Going into the decade of the 1960s, the Delta region was also not much different than the Old South in other aspects: Jim Crow laws of racial segregation ruled the region; more than half of blacks more than 30 years old had less than a seventh grade education, with the state spending less than one-quarter the money per black student than it did per white student and black teachers earning less than half their white counterparts; blacks job opportunities remained overwhelmingly in unskilled, agricultural labor; and less than 5 percent of eligible blacks were registered to vote.[17]

It was in this Delta region that Lusia Harris was born to Willie and Ethel Harris in Minter City, Mississippi, in 1955. Minter City is a small town just north of Greenwood, the center of the Mississippi cotton trade and self-proclaimed "Long-Staple Cotton Capital of the World."[18] Harris was the tenth of 11 children and, like most African American families in this region, each had to work and contribute to the household's welfare. Harris attended high school at Amanda Elzy High School in Greenwood, where she starred on the basketball team. On graduating from Elzy in 1973, Harris got the opportunity to continue her basketball career at nearby Delta State University in Cleveland, Mississippi.

Although Delta State was close to home, Harris's decision to attend school there was somewhat of a surprise. In the context of racial mores, the state of Mississippi and the Delta region had not changed dramatically by the early 1970s when compared to the tumultuous decade of the 1960s. This region was steeped in a tradition that basically precluded black and white interaction on an equal basis, and sudden changes in laws could not revise perceptions, tendencies, and comfort levels between the races. In higher education specifically, James Meredith's successful attempt to desegregate the University of Mississippi in 1962 was a critical breakthrough to truly obey the Brown decision, yet it did not result in an immediate transition in the racial diversity of state-funded institutions in Mississippi. By the early 1970s, African American representation in Mississippi colleges and universities beyond the historically black schools was still extremely low.

Nevertheless, Harris was interested in playing basketball in college, so when the opportunity to attend Delta State was made available, she took it. Harris recalls the shock of the transition from all-black Elzy High School to often being the only African American in a class stating, "And it was a big adjustment for me because I had to adjust to being in a different environment. You know, it was totally different."[19] Despite this major adjustment, Harris developed meaningful relationships with her college peers.

Harris's ability to be accepted was certainly influenced by her presence on the emerging Delta State women's basketball team. The Lady Statesmen were led by legendary women's coach Lily Margaret Wade. Recognized as "the mother of modern women's basketball," Wade took over the program at Delta State where she had played 40 years earlier.[20] Women's college basketball was at a critical juncture in the early 1970s, as Congress had just adopted Title IX in 1972, prohibiting sex discrimination in women's sports. The year before Title IX was adopted, a new organization, the Association for Intercollegiate Athletics for Women (AIAW), was formed to govern women's athletics at the college level.

The timing of AIAW oversight, Wade's leadership, and Harris's arrival on campus in 1973 combined to put the Lady Statesmen women's basketball team immediately in the national spotlight. Beginning with the 1974–75 season, Harris's sophomore year, the Lady Statesmen achieved a phenomenal record of 93 wins and only 4 losses. More impressive is winning the AIAW National Championship three consecutive years. Harris was clearly the star of the team—she was a three-time All-American; she was the starting center on the first U.S. women's basketball Olympic team in 1976; she held 15 of 18 Delta State team, single game and career records; and she finished her career averaging almost 26 points and 15 rebounds per game. Other impressive accolades for Harris include scoring the first basket in history for U.S. women's Olympic basketball, being the first women to be drafted by the National Basketball Association in 1977 (New Orleans Jazz), and being enshrined into several Halls of Fame.[21]

Harris's individual and team accomplishments rank her high on the list of women who have helped bring respect and notoriety to women's basketball. By the early 1980s, women's participation in college basketball and numerous other sports were being incorporated into the fabric of the National Collegiate Athletic Association. This would lead to the demise of the AIAW, but its existence and success had spearheaded the push for respectability for women's collegiate athletics.

Although Harris's impressive credentials as a basketball player brought her and Delta State national recognition, her contributions do not seem to have been acknowledged through the lens of civil rights. But in analyzing Harris in the context of the era and region in which she became a nationally known sports star, one word describes her contributions to women's sports and society—pioneer. There are at least three interrelated reasons that help explain why Harris is not necessarily considered in the category of civil rights advocate. First, as an admittedly private, introspective person, Harris was not one to lead marches or speak out about an injustice she may have experienced or witnessed. Even when asked about discrimination that she faced, Harris responded dismissively by stating, "Minor things. Sometimes the fans would say, you know, things in the stands, but my focus was to score that basket, and not focus on things that were happening in the stands because, you know, we had no control over that."[22] It is not clear what Harris means by "minor things," but when derogatory comments or actions occur, especially in public places, they can no longer be considered minor. More likely, Harris just chose to ignore them and focus on the task at hand. Her individual and team performances suggest that she was quite apt at keeping focused.

Second, by the mid-1970s, the United States wanted to focus on other issues beyond civil rights for African Americans. The 1960s had provided numerous embarrassing moments for the country and too much violence had occurred, ranging from the bus bombings and physical beatings experienced by Student Nonviolent Coordinating Committee early in the decade, to the assassination of Dr. Martin Luther King Jr. at the end. The country could also point to tangible signs of having solved the racial injustice problem in the 1960s, as the Civil Rights and Voting Rights Acts that were passed in the mid-1960s were watershed declarations. Combined with examples of the implementation of the Brown decision, this translated into social, political, and educational equality for all Americans. Almost as a part of our country's maturation process, people wanted to turn to others areas in which to improve.

Third, Harris broke racial ground on the basketball court and beyond at Delta State. Despite her individual and team success, looking at the team photographs of the three, consecutive AIAW champions reveals that Harris remained the only black player on the Delta State women's basketball team. Perhaps there were no other Lusia Harrises out there to recruit, but it is difficult to imagine that such success would not inspire talented black high school stars to want to play with Harris at Delta State. Similarly, the demographics of the school were not unlike most others schools in the South. In both elementary schools and colleges and universities, blacks and whites continued to exist in segregated school systems. Yet apparently the class that Harris exuded as a player was recognized by her peers beyond the court. In 1976, much to her surprise, Harris was voted homecoming queen at Delta State. Winning this recognition came as a complete surprise to Harris, who, as a 6'3" African American basketball player, defied the stereotypical look of the homecoming queen at a white Southern university. Breaking new ground in this context was a significant step in meeting Dr. King's desire to have people judged by the content of their character rather than the color of their skin.

Lusia Harris is not likely to be mentioned as a civil rights crusader on many people's lists. In fact, there is no evidence to suggest that Harris would even agree that such a title is appropriate for her. But whether or not Harris intentionally raised the consciousness of race and gender equity is not important. What is important is that Harris's success as an athlete and the regard that people had for her as a person helped pave a road that would produce clear signs of progress for blacks and women in sports for the last quarter of the twentieth century.

As time passed and the United States could point to more "firsts" for African Americans in sports, it became much easier to distance itself from the racial tumult, conflict, and limitations that defined society and athletics for most of the century. The path-forging legal changes of the 1950s and 1960s, followed by occasional examples of blacks who broke barriers in sports and elsewhere, has gone a long way toward freeing America of its guilty conscious. One does not have to look far to prove the preponderance of such sentiment.

For example, the Civil Rights Act of 1964 is credited with bringing about substantive increases in job and educational opportunities for

African Americans. Title XII, which was the foundation for affirmative action initiatives, led to intentional efforts for more blacks gaining entry into corporate America and politics, as well as first-time access into many white colleges and universities by the 1970s. These programs resulted in blacks holding positions usually reserved for whites. Given the nation's track record in this regard, any presence of blacks in corporate executive jobs, positions of political leadership, or acceptance into elite graduate school programs was noticeable. With this newfound presence, much of America could believe that racial-based inequities, although not necessarily forgotten, could at least be considered incidents of the past. And as every trickle of progress occurred, the nation could reduce the significance of race being tied to opportunity and people could be judged simply on their merit.

This way of thinking could also turn to the sports world for reinforcement. In the 1970s and 1980s, much like in the economic, political, and educational arenas, African Americans gained prominence in several sports that had traditionally seemed reserved for whites. In particular, Arthur Ashe became the first African American man to win the prestigious Wimbledon tournament in 1975 and captain of the Davis Cup team from 1981 to 1985; women's volleyball star Flora Hyman, who helped put American women's volleyball on the international map in the late 1970s, was the undeniable team leader and best player of the Olympic team that won the silver medal in 1984 in Los Angeles, California; and in 1988 figure skater Debi Thomas, dubbed "America's Sweetheart," won a bronze medal at the Olympic Games to become the first African American to win a medal in the Winter Games. The success of these great athletes contributed to the declining significance of race in the sports world which, in turn, was transferable to society at-large. Beyond their accomplishments in their respective sports, Ashe, Hyman, and Thomas maintained profiles that made race more easily forgettable: All three evoked national patriotism and loyalty by representing the country internationally with pride and without much controversy; each was very well educated, which meshes nicely with the notion that hard work is the decisive key to success in sports and beyond; and each, if they decided to question the influence of race in America, did so in an acceptable manner of intellectual exchange and dialogue. Throughout the post-Civil Rights movement era, evidence of tangible progress in athletics and beyond has allowed most Americans, regardless of race, to diminish the preoccupation with race that historically has dominated our nation's existence.

It is within this backdrop that Venus and Serena Williams emerged onto the national radar in the sport of tennis. Beginning in July 1990, with an article in *The New York Times* and followed by a front-page story in *Time* in early 1991, the Williams sisters had a compelling story for the nation to hear. In essence, they were poor, urban girls interested in tennis and fortunate enough to have a father who made extreme sacrifices to support his daughters in their desire to become tennis stars.[23] Although some criticized Richard Williams for perhaps pushing his daughters too hard, most accepted him as the stereotypical "tennis parent" who was notorious for being possessive and obsessive. Overall, it was not surprising that this story had so much national appeal. The Williams sisters represented what many Americans wanted to believe—that if an individual works hard and sacrifices enough s/he can accomplish even the most unexpected. Thus impoverished, African American girls can become tennis stars. Essentially, the Williams sisters were "pulling themselves up by their bootstraps" to become a Horatio Alger story of the late twentieth century.

Although it was an inspiring story, it was not realistic. Only a handful of African America men or women had ever reached any degree of notoriety on the professional tennis circuit, and it had been the mid-1950s since a black woman, Althea Gibson, had come close to dominating tennis. But the Williams sisters and their parents, Richard and Oracene, continued to plug along, and by the late-1990s, it was apparent that national tennis stardom was in the future for both Venus and Serena. Venus, who turned professional on January 1, 1994, signed a five-year $12 million contract with Reebok in 1995, and Serena made her professional debut in 1997 and signed a similar contract with Puma in 1998. Deals of this sort were very unusual for female tennis players, particularly those unproven in the professional ranks. Such financial endorsements combined with a barrage of media attention to prove that these two young African American women had captivated the country.

So the question remains, "Why?" There had always been young and promising American tennis players who the country wished well. In fact, women's tennis is known for placing enormous pressure on girls at an early age to take the tennis world by storm. But to provide a woman player with financial security within a year of becoming a professional player and without any tournament titles under her belt basically was unfamiliar territory for the tennis establishment. Nevertheless, this is exactly the situation that the Williams sisters enjoyed.

The answer rests not in any individual explanation, but in a combination of factors, the most important of which have been mentioned—their talent, their background, and their race. These intriguing factors captured America during an era when it could embrace all three at the same time for the first time. Although Venus and Serena had not produced yet on the professional circuit, their talent was undeniable. This had been confirmed by legendary players such as Billie Jean King, who claimed that "the girls possess aggressiveness and a volleying aptitude beyond their years."[24] Their background of coming from less-than-privileged social status was combined with four years of premier training at Rick Macci's tennis academy in Florida. As well, it had been 40 years since greatness had been achieved in tennis by an African American woman, and the Williams sisters had displayed enough promise to convince people that they were the best candidates to come along.

The combination of these factors makes the generous offers extended to Venus and Serena by Reebok and Puma seem like rather safe bets. From a marketing perspective, talent, background, and race covered a multitude of interests nationally. Traditionalists in the tennis world are always thinking about issues like the next generation of stars and maintaining the integrity of the game. America was proud to have in the national spotlight examples that reinforced its founding principles. The presence of African American tennis stars brought in an untapped demographic market in black people, whose value and interest in athletics was already recognized. These factors culminated into a calculated risk that any successful athletic shoe and apparel company would welcome.

What Reebok and Puma already knew, the rest of the public would soon find out. Venus and Serena burst onto the tennis scene in 1999. In June they combined to become the first sisters to win a doubles title in the twentieth century by winning the French Open. Five months later Serena followed this victory by winning the sisters' first Grand Slam singles title at the U.S. Open. Venus would soon catch up as she won Wimbledon, the U.S. Open, and the Olympics in 2000. Her spectacular year culminated in being named Sports Illustrated for Women Sportswoman of the Year. Venus followed this special year by repeating at Wimbledon and the U.S. Open. The U.S. Open was special for other reasons—she met her sister Serena in the finals, marking the first time siblings had met in 117 years, and the finals match between them was broadcasted on television in prime time.[25] The decision to air a tennis match at peak viewing time epitomized the popularity and interest generated by these two sisters. Surely a part of why this happened was that they were sisters competing for the most coveted prize in tennis on American soil, and people were curious to see how each player would perform in this history-making match.

Yet even with so much success and attention, the Williams sisters endured harsh feedback and commentary. From one perspective, one could conclude that the criticism directed at Venus and Serena just came with the territory of being high-profile players. At the same time, they were known to be the subject of derogatory comments that other players did not receive. For example, tennis commentators such as Chris Everett, John McEnroe, and Tracy Austin often described Venus and Serena after matches as sloppy, careless, or that they relied too much on their athletic ability rather than playing the game correctly.[26] These words are not particularly denigrating critiques, but they were sometimes used even after victories. The sisters have also been the victims of more personal and aggressive criticism that had nothing to do with their inadequacies as players. The most memorable of these attacks came in June of 2001. Sid Rosenberg, a white radio sportscaster in New York City, was fired for reportedly calling Venus Williams an "animal" while on air. In sports, being called an animal is not inherently negative, as it sometimes speaks to an athlete's tenacity and desire to win. But on this particular occasion, Rosenberg eliminated this particular rationale for his comment by further stating that Venus and Serena had a better chance of posing nude for *National Geographic* than for *Playboy*.[27]

When suggestions were made that his comments were racist, Rosenberg stated that "nothing could be further from the truth."[28] He went on to apologize on the air and reportedly sent a letter of apology to the two sisters. He was also rehired in the same job at the same radio station. Perhaps Rosenberg meant nothing by his comments and was sorry that he had offended Venus and Serena. It is also possible that the Williams sisters truly forgave him for suggesting that they were animals rather than human beings. Still, given America's discomfort with its racial past and the chattel-like role that many black women were known to have experienced, Rosenberg's comments pricked a very slow-healing wound that runs deep in our country.

Whenever an incident like this happens, people are usually expected to fall into one of two categories—the group that says "stop being so sensitive; he didn't mean anything by it," or the groups that contends "he is a racist and he needs to suffer the most severe penalty possible." Perhaps both or neither perspective is true. What is important is that regardless of how many times situations like this take place, African American women athletes have a legacy of continuing to bounce back; they continue to compete; they continue to excel; they continue to inspire the next generation of black female athletes. The achievements of women such as Wilma Rudolph, Lusia Harris, and Venus and Serena Williams are significant not because we should relish in the past, but because by acknowledging their accomplishments, we already have a road map of what is to come in the future.

AFTERWORD

Since I began writing this book, there have been more than a few significant breakthroughs for African Americans in the world of athletics—yet none rank higher than the racial barriers toppled by two schools in the Southeastern Conference (SEC). In December 2003, the University of Georgia and Mississippi State University hired black men to prominent positions historically held by whites. At the University of Georgia, Damon Evans was named director of athletics, and at Mississippi State University, Sylvester Croom was named head football coach. At the press conferences announcing their hires, both men were careful to emphasize the task at hand in their respective jobs rather than their racial identity. But one cannot help but believe that Evans and Croom understood the magnitude of these decisions. At the very least, Evans and Croom were aware that getting such sacred positions in the world of college athletics in the south means that almost anything is possible in the twenty-first century. To truly understand this occasion, one only needs to consider how preoccupied southerners are with sports, particularly college football. In a typical college football season, rarely does an SEC team play games in front of less than capacity crowds, and most schools expect their athletic departments to be profitable. In other words, for the overwhelming majority of SEC institutions, football has a religion-like fervor, and closely aligned to this energy are the financial resources associated with it.

Prior to Evans and Croom, most people assumed that positions such as athletic director and head football coach were too high profile and important to institutional stability to risk having African Americans at the helm. Thus, explanations such as "we need someone with more experience" or "he just wasn't the right fit" became code language for off-limits—blacks need not apply. In the case of Croom, he experienced a version of these excuses from his alma mater, the University of Alabama. A native of Tuscaloosa, Alabama, and an all-American player at the University of Alabama under legendary coach Paul "Bear" Bryant, Croom had served as an assistant coach at his alma mater for 11 years and for 17 years in professional football. The school also named an award in his honor, which was given annually to the team's outstanding player. But when the university had the opportunity to hire Croom as its head football coach, they opted to hire another former player, Mike Shula. Not that Shula was an inappropriate choice but, in essence, Croom was another in the long line of black coaches determined to be "not the right fit." Nevertheless, Croom got his chance when Mississippi State University offered him the position.

Because of the longstanding practice of overlooking African American candidates, many were surprised when the University of Georgia opted to hire Evans as the school's athletic director. High-profile positions such as this almost always go to more experienced athletic administrators with more tangible accomplishments. But with the endorsement of longtime football coach and out-going athletic director Vince Dooley, Evans's limited experience was not a deterrent. Evans has hit the ground running in his new role and embarked on an unprecedented $60 million capital campaign for the school's athletic association.

Much like the African American sports pioneers who came before them, Evans and Croom face added pressures as "firsts" in their positions. Hopefully when times are tough, they will gain strength by reflecting on the strength and persistence practiced by previous black path breakers in sport. As well, I hope that Evans, Croom, and others represent a future where their failures and successes in the office and on the field will be the true measuring stick by which they are judged.

NOTES

CAN THEY REALLY PLAY? AFRICAN AMERICAN PARTICIPATION IN "WHITE" SPORTS

1. W.E.B. Du Bois, "Talented Tenth," in *The Negro Problem: A Series of Articles by Representative Negroes of To-Day* (New York: James Pott and Co., 1903).

2. This background for perceptions of blacks in America is best described in Winthrop Jordan, *White Over Black: American Attitudes Toward the Negro, 1550–1812* (New York: W. W. Norton, 1968).

3. U. B. Phillips, *American Negro Slavery: A Survey of the Supply, Employment, and Control of Negro Labor as Determined by the Plantation Regime* (Baton Rough, La.: State University Press, 1966).

4. David Roediger, *The Wages of Whiteness: Race and the Making of the American Working Class* (London and New York: Verso, 1991).

5. Edward Hotaling, *The Great Black Jockeys: The Lives and Times of the Men Who Dominated America's First National Sport* (Rocklin, Ca.: Forum, Prima Publishing, 1999).

6. Ibid., 177–178.

7. Ibid., 225.

8. Ibid., 209–239.

9. David Wiggins, "Isaac Murphy: Black Hero in Nineteenth-Century American Sport, 1861–1896," in *Glory Bound: Black Athletes in a White America*

(Syracuse, N.Y.: Syracuse University Press, 1997), 21–33; Arthur Ashe, *A Hard Road to Glory: A History of the African-American Athlete, 1619–1918* (New York: Amistad, 1988), 48.

10. Hotaling, 311–340.

11. Calvin Sinnette, *Forbidden Fairways: African Americans and the Game of Golf* (Chelsea, Mich.: Sleeping Bear Press, 1998), 7–34.

12. Ibid.

13. William Tuttle, *Race Riot: Chicago in the Red Summer of 1919* (Urbana: University of Illinois Press, 1970), 157–183.

14. Ibid., 125.

15. Ibid., 12–15.

16. Ibid., 30–34.

17. Ibid., 78–90.

18. Brian McFarlane, *History of Hockey* (Champaign, Ill.: Sports Publishing, Inc., 1997).

19. Herb Carnegie, *A Fly In a Pail of Milk: The Herb Carnegie Story* (Ontario-New York: Mosaic Press, 1997), 22–23.

20. Ibid., 104–115.

21. Ibid., 125.

22. Ibid., 57.

23. Ibid., 133.

24. Jimmy Golen, "NHL Honors Willie O'Ree, League's First Black Player," *Associated Press*, March 25, 2003, 1–3.

25. Golen, 1–3.

26. Ed Willes, "Belated Credit for a Goal: After 40 Years, the NHL Recognizes Its First Black Player," *New York Times*, January 19, 1998, C23; Golen, 1–3.

27. Golen, 1.

28. Donald Jacobs, "The Nineteenth Century Struggle over Segregated Education in the Boston Schools," *Journal of Negro Education* 39 (Winter, 1970), 76–85.

29. Ron Thomas, *They Cleared the Lane: The NBA's Black Pioneers* (Lincoln: University of Nebraska Press, 2002), 26–27.

30. Al Hirshberg, *What's the Matter with the Red Sox* (New York: Dodd, Mead, and Company, 1973), 143.

31. ATA—Black Tennis Mecca. Available at http://www.atanational.com/about.htm.

32. Ibid.

33. Althea Gibson, *I Always Wanted to Be Somebody* (New York: Harper, 1958).

HEROES OR VILLAINS? THE CATEGORIZATION OF AFRICAN AMERICAN STAR ATHLETES, 1892–1946

1. Michael Eric Dyson, "Be Like Mike? Michael Jordan and the Pedagogy of Desire," *Cultural Studies 7* (January 1993), 64–72.

2. Located in David Wiggins and Patrick Miller, *An Unlevel Playing Field: A Documentary History of the African American Experience in Sport* (Urbana: University of Illinois Press, 2003), 71–73; "Lewis' Great Work," *AME Zion Quarterly Review 10* (October–December 1900), 63–64.

3. Harold Wade, Jr., *Black Men of Amherst* (Amherst, Mass.: Amherst College Press, 1976).

4. Louis Harlan, *Booker T. Washington: The Wizard of Tuskegee, 1901–1915* (New York: Oxford University Press, 1983), 348.

5. Louis Harlan, *Booker T. Washington: The Making of a Black Leader, 1856–1901* (New York: Oxford University Press, 1972).

6. Harlan, *Booker T. Washington: The Wizard of Tuskegee*, 17.

7. Harold Wade, *Black Men of Amherst* (Amherst, Mass.: Amherst College Press, 1976), 67.

8. Harlan, *Booker T. Washington: The Wizard of Tuskegee*, 48.

9. Wade, 68.

10. Ibid.

11. Al-Tony Gilmore, *Bad Nigger! The National Impact of Jack Johnson* (New York: Kennikat, 1975).

12. Robert Zangrando, *The NAACP Crusade Against Lynching, 1909–1950* (Philadelphia: Temple University Press, 1980).

13. In Wiggins and Miller, 81–82; W.E.B. Du Bois, "The Prizefighter," *Crisis 8* (August 1914), 181.

14. Gilmore, "Jack Johnson and White Women: The National Impact," *Journal of Negro History*, 58, no. 1 (January 1973): 19.

15. Ibid. Quote reprinted in *Fort Worth Citizen Star*, October 24, 1912.

16. Louis Harlan, ed., *The Booker T. Washington Papers* (Urbana: University of Illinois Press, 1982), vol. 12, 43–44.

17. Martin Duberman, *Paul Robeson: A Biography* (New York: The New Press, 1989), 10.

18. Ibid., 12–16.

19. Paul Robeson with Lloyd Brown, *Here I Stand* (Boston: Beacon Press, 1958), 20.

20. Duberman, 17.

21. Ibid., 20.

22. Ibid.

23. Ibid.

24. Ibid., 26.

25. Jeffrey Stewart, ed. *Paul Robeson: Artist and Citizen* (Rutgers University Press, 1998), 81.

26. Duberman, 301.

27. Ibid., 344.

28. Ibid., 27.

29. Stewart, 45–46.

WHEN THE ROOSTER CROWS: AFRICAN AMERICAN ATHLETES IN THE STRUGGLE FOR CIVIL RIGHTS, 1954–1968

1. *New York Times*, Feb. 28, 1964.

2. Robert Cook, *Sweet Land of Liberty? The African-American Struggle for Civil Rights in the Twentieth Century* (London and New York: Longman, 1998), 39.

3. David Wiggins, *Glory Bound: Black Athletes in a White America* (Syracuse, N.Y.: Syracuse University Press, 1997), chapter 6.

4. Bill Russell and Taylor Branch, *Second Wind: The Memoirs of an Opinionated Man* (New York: Random House, 1979), 210–212.

5. Ibid., 211.

6. Ibid., 198.

7. Ibid., 3.

8. Ibid., 10.

9. Ibid., chapter 5.

10. Ron Thomas, *They Cleared the Lane: The NBAs Black Pioneers* (Lincoln: University of Nebraska Press, 2002), 177.

11. Ron Flatter, *Russell Was Proud, Fierce Warrior* (2003). Available at http://espn.go.com/sportscentury/features/00016449.html.

12. Jimmy Brown with Myron Cope, *Off My Chest* (Garden City, N.J.: Doubleday and Company, 1964), 163.

13. Ibid., 98–102.

14. David Wiggins and Patrick Miller, *An Unlevel Playing Field: A Documentary History of the African American Experience in Sport* (Urbana: University of Illinois Press, 2003), 343.

15. Brown, 117.

16. Ibid., 130.

17. Ibid., 102.

18. Miller and Wiggins, 343.

19. Brown, 164.

20. Miller and Wiggins, 343.

21. To fully understand the rules of segregation and professional football, see Charles Ross, *Outside the Lines: African Americans and the Integration of the National Football League* (New York: New York University Press, 1999).

22. Thomas Smith, "Outside the Pale: The Exclusion of Blacks from the National Football League, 1934–1946," *Journal of Sport History* 15 (Winter, 1988), 278.

23. *New York Times*, February 27, 1964.

24. *New York Times*, February 28, 1964

25. *New York Times*, March 7, 1964.

26. *Miami Herald*, February 7, 1964.

27. *New York Times*, February 28, 1964.

28. The two best studies on Muhammad Ali's life and boxing career are Thomas Hauser, *Muhammad Ali: His Life and Times* (New York: Simon and Schuster, 1991), and Elliot Gorn, ed., *Muhammad Ali: The People's Champ* (Urbana: University of Illinois Press, 1995).

29. *New York Times*, April 29, 1967.

30. *Sports Illustrated*, June 1, 1967.

31. David Wiggins, *Glory Bound*, 104–122.

THE RULES HAVE CHANGED BUT THE GAME IS STILL THE SAME: BLACK ATHLETES' ACHIEVEMENTS IN THE CIVIL RIGHTS ERA AND BEYOND

1. Harry Edwards, *The Revolt of the Black Athlete* (New York: Free Press, 1969), 38–43.

2. Jack Scott, "The White Olympics," *Ramparts* 6 (May), 59.

3. Curt Flood with Richard Carter, *Curt Flood: The Way It Is* (New York: Trident Press, 1971), 23.

4. Ibid., 27.

5. Ibid., 37.

6. Ibid., 39–41.

7. Ibid., 27.

8. William Van Deburg, *New Day in Babylon: The Black Power Movement and American Culture, 1965–1975* (Chicago and London: University of Chicago Press, 1992), 129.

9. For a good summary of the Civil Rights movement, see Harvard Sitkoff, *The Struggle for Black Equality, 1954–1992* (New York: Hill and Wang, 1993).

10. Deburg, *New Day in Bablyon*, 32–34.

11. Nick Acoccella, "Robinson Set Records and Broke Barriers," *ESPN.com*, 1–4.

12. *BaseballLibrary.com*, 1–10.

13. Ibid.

14. Ibid.

15. Acoccella, *ESPN.com*, 1–4.

16. Ibid.

17. "In America's National Pastime, Says Frank Robinson, White Is the Color of the Game off the Field," *People Weekly*, April 27, 1987.

18. Ibid.

19. Phil Petrie, "The NFL Sacks the Black Quarterback," *Encore American and Worldwide News*, October 18, 1976, 323–327.

20. Ibid.

21. Ibid.

22. David Roediger, *Colored White: Transcending the Racial Past* (Berkeley: University of California Press, 2002), with Leola Johnson, "Hertz, Don't It?": White "Colorblindness" and the Marketing of O. J. Simpson," 69.

23. Lawrence Linderman and Fred Robbins, "O. J. Simpson: a Candid Conversation with the Best-Liked, Best-Paid Football Player Ever," *Playboy Magazine*, 1976.

24. Doug Williams with Bruce Hunter, *QuarterBlack: Shattering the NFL Myth* (Chicago: Bonus Books, 1990), 170.

25. Ibid.

"SHE'S DONE MORE FOR HER COUNTRY THAN WHAT THE U.S. COULD HAVE PAID HER FOR": AFRICAN AMERICAN WOMAN AND SPORTS

1. Deborah Gray White, *Ar'n't I a Woman?: Female Slaves in the Plantation South* (New York and London: W. W. Norton & Company, 1985), 14.

2. Ibid.

3. Patricia Vertinsky and Gwendolyn Captain, "More Myth than History: American Culture and Representations of the Black Female's Athletic Ability," *Journal of Sport History* 25 (Fall 1998), 532–561.

4. White, *Ar'n't I a Woman?*, 15.

5. Rosalyn Terborg-Penn, *African American Women in the Struggle for the Vote, 1850–1920* (Bloomington and Indianapolis: Indiana University Press, 1998), 36.

6. Susan Cahn, *Coming on Strong: Gender and Sexuality in Twentieth-Century Women's Sport* (New York: The Free Press, 1994), 118.

7. Ibid., 118.

8. Alex Haley, "The Queen Who Earned Her Crown," *The Rotarian* (May 1961), found in Patrick Miller and David K. Wiggins, *The Unlevel Playing Field: A Documentary History of the African American Experience in Sport* (Urbana and Chicago: University of Illinois Press, 2003), 263–268. Also see, M. B. Roberts, "Rudolph Ran and the World Went Wild," *ESPN.com* (2005), 1–4.

9. Haley in Miller and Wiggins, *The Unlevel Playing Field*, 267.

10. Roberts, *ESPN.com*, 4.

11. Cahn, *Coming on Strong*, 125.

12. Haley in Miller and Wiggins, *The Unlevel Playing Field*, 268.

13. Roberts, *ESPN.com*, 3.

14. Ibid., 3.

15. Belinda Robnett, *How Long? How Long?: African-American Women in the Struggle for Civil Rights* (New York: Oxford University Press, 1997), 87–97.

16. Chana Lee, *for freedom's sake: The Life of Fannie Lou Hamer* (Urbana and Chicago: University of Illinois Press, 1999), 1.

17. Charles Payne, *I've Got the Light of Freedom: The Organizing Tradition and the Mississippi Freedom Struggle* (Berkeley: University of California Press, 1995), 16–20.

18. John Dittmer, *Local People: The Struggle for Civil Rights in Mississippi* (Urbana: University of Illinois, 1995), 128.

19. Interview with Lusia Harris-Stewart, *Mississippi Oral History Project* (University of Southern Mississippi), December 18, 1999.

20. "Lily Margaret Wade," *GoStatesmen.com*.

21. Interview with Lusia Harris-Stewart, *Mississippi Oral History Project*.

22. Ibid.

23. "Status: Undefeated. Future: Rosy. Age: 10," *The New York Times*, July 3, 1990.

24. Quote from King on April 5, 1992, *SI.com*.

25. Ibid., September 8, 2001.

26. Mariah Burton Nelson, "Sisters Show How to Compete—And Care," *Newsday* (September 11, 2001).

27. "Fired White Sportscaster Apologizes for Remarks about Venus and Serena Williams; Gets Rehired," *Jet* (July 9, 2001).

28. Ibid.

SELECTED BIBLIOGRAPHY

PUBLISHED SOURCES

Ashe, Arthur. A *Hard Road to Glory: A History of the African-American Athlete, 1619–1918*. New York: Amistad, 1988.

Brown, Jimmy with Cope, Myron. *Off My Chest*. Garden City, N.J.: Doubleday and Company, 1964.

Cahn, Susan. *Coming on Strong: Gender and Sexuality in Twentieth-Century Women's Sport*. New York: The Free Press, 1994.

Carnegie, Herb. *A Fly in a Pail of Milk: The Herb Carnegie Story*. Ontario-New York: Mosaic Press, 1997.

Dittmer, John. *Local People: The Struggle for Civil Rights in Mississippi*. Urbana: University of Illinois, 1995.

Duberman, Martin. *Paul Robeson: A Biography*. New York: The New Press, 1989.

Edwards, Harry. *The Revolt of the Black Athlete*. New York: Free Press, 1969.

Flood, Curt with Carter, Richard. *Curt Flood: The Way It Is*. New York: Trident Press, 1971.

Gibson, Althea. *I Always Wanted to Be Somebody*. New York: Harper, 1958.

Gilmore, Al-Tony. *Bad Nigger! The National Impact of Jack Johnson*. New York: Kennikat, 1975.

Harlan, Louis. *Booker T. Washington: The Wizard of Tuskegee, 1901–1915*. New York: Oxford University Press, 1983.

Hotaling, Edward. *The Great Black Jockeys: The Lives and Times of the Men Who Dominated America's First National Sport*. Rocklin, Ca.: Forum, Prima Publishing, 1999.

Payne, Charles. *I've Got the Light of Freedom: The Organizing Tradition and the Mississippi Freedom Struggle*. Berkeley: University of California Press, 1995.

Robnett, Belinda. *How Long? How Long?: African-American Women in the Struggle for Civil Rights*. New York: Oxford University Press, 1997.

Russell, Bill and Branch, Taylor. *Second Wind: The Memoirs of an Opinionated Man*. New York: Random House, 1979.

Sinnette, Calvin. *Forbidden Fairways: African Americans and the Game of Golf*. Chelsea, Mich.: Sleeping Bear Press, 1998.

Stewart, Jeffrey, ed. *Paul Robeson: Artist and Citizen*. New Brunswick, N.J.: Rutgers University Press, 1998.

Terborg-Penn, Rosalyn. *African American Women in the Struggle for the Vote, 1850–1920*. Bloomington and Indianapolis: Indiana University Press, 1998.

Van Deburg, William. *New Day in Babylon: The Black Power Movement and American Culture, 1965–1975*. Chicago and London: University of Chicago Press, 1992.

Wade Jr., Harold. *Black Men of Amherst*. Amherst College Press 1976.

White, Deborah Gray. *Ar'n't I a Woman?: Female Slaves in the Plantation South*. New York: W.W. Norton & Company, 1985.

Wiggins, David. *Glory Bound: Black Athletes in a White America*. Syracuse, N.Y.: Syracuse University Press, 1997.

Wiggins, David and Miller, Patrick. *An Unlevel Playing Field: A Documentary History of the African American Experience in Sport*. Urbana: University of Illinois Press, 2003.

INDEX

About the Author

RUSSELL T. WIGGINTON is Vice-President for College Relations at Rhodes College in Memphis, Tennessee, and former Assistant Professor of History at Rhodes College.